Mark Twain's
Burlesque Patterns

Mark Twain's
Burlesque Patterns

As Seen in the
Novels and Narratives
1855-1885

FRANKLIN R. ROGERS

SOUTHERN METHODIST UNIVERSITY PRESS, DALLAS
1960

Published with the Assistance of a Grant
From the Ford Foundation
Under Its Program for the Support of Publication
In the Humanities and Social Sciences

Library of Congress Catalog Card Number: 60-15893

Printed in the United States of America at Dallas, Texas

Preface

WITH A VIEW similar to Miss Gladys C. Bellamy's in *Mark Twain as a Literary Artist,* that Twain was "much more the conscious craftsman than is generally believed," I began the present study as a doctoral dissertation at the University of California, Berkeley, and pursued it beyond the dissertation stage in hopes of supplementing the critic's and the literary historian's knowledge of Mark Twain's craftsmanship. Because a study of all elements of literary craftsmanship in sufficient detail to demonstrate a coherent development would involve a volume of gigantic proportions, I have focused upon Twain's structural patterns, turning to style and characterization only insofar as these elements are pertinent to the major purpose. In the course of the study the fact that Mark Twain's apprenticeship in burlesque was the major shaping influence upon the novelist produced a further sharpening of the thesis.

Because the focus of the study is Twain's structural patterns derived from burlesque, I have had to limit both the denotation and the connotation of at least one word central to the study: *burlesque.* Throughout the text, except in quotations from other critics or in instances where another application is specifically indicated, *burlesque* refers only to literary burlesque, a humorous imitation and exaggeration of the conventions in plot, characterization, and style peculiar to a literary type, the works of a certain author, or a particular book, play, short story, or poem. In an effort to gain greater precision in description, I have used the term *parody-burlesque* or simply *parody* to designate that type of bur-

v

lesque in which the principal means of achieving humor is a ludicrous exaggeration of the target author's stylistic mannerisms. Finally, for the sake of convenience, I have used the phrase *travel-burlesque* to designate a burlesque of travel literature as a genre.

The words *burlesque* and *parody* generally connote a critical or satirical attitude on the part of the writer toward the target, but I have attempted to avoid such a connotation in my thinking not only because of my desire to concentrate upon the purely technical in the construction of the narratives and novels written prior to 1885 but also because of other reasons specified in the study. In applying the terms to various works by Twain I have had no wish to imply a critical or satirical intent behind the works in question.

I wish to acknowledge the kindness of the following publishers who have granted me permission to use copyrighted materials: Harper and Brothers and The Huntington Library for quotations from the works of Mark Twain, and Charles Scribner's Sons for a quotation from *The Tocsin of Revolt and Other Essays* by Brander Matthews. Passages from "The Boy's Manuscript" are reprinted by permission of the publishers from Bernard DeVoto, *Mark Twain at Work,* Cambridge, Mass.: Harvard University Press, copyright 1942 by the President and Fellows of Harvard College. To the Mark Twain Company and the New York Public Library (Henry W. and Albert A. Berg Collection), I am grateful for permission to quote from the unpublished manuscripts of Mark Twain.

For aid in checking various details pertinent to the study, I wish to thank Kenneth I. Pettitt of the Yale University Library; the staff of the Bancroft Library, especially Helen Bretnor; and Frederick Anderson, assistant to the editor of the Mark Twain Papers.

I am especially grateful to Henry Nash Smith, whose counsel as director of the dissertation and generosity as editor of the Mark Twain Papers have left me completely in his debt. I wish also to thank Walter Blair, of the University of Chicago, who read an early draft of the section on *Huckleberry Finn* and offered criticisms which have contributed greatly to that portion of the study. Both

Mr. Blair and Mr. Smith were generous not only with advice and criticisms but also with material aid, permitting me to read manuscripts of studies not yet published at that time and calling my attention to pertinent passages in the Mark Twain Papers which I had either overlooked or not yet encountered.

For a different but no less important encouragement and aid, I am indebted to my wife, who has willingly suffered much of the drudgery connected with such an undertaking as this.

FRANKLIN R. ROGERS

Milwaukee, Wisconsin
July 8, 1960

Contents

Mark Twain's Burlesque Patterns

1

Burlesque:
A Route to the Craft of Fiction

IN HIS early years as a writer, Samuel L. Clemens produced a large number of tales, anecdotes, sketches, and articles. From these ephemera emerged Mark Twain, the novelist and artist, but just how or why the emergence occurred has been the subject of much discussion. One popular view, denying that he developed at all, regards him, to use Arnold Bennett's phrase, as "a divine amateur." Those who hold that his development involved more than mere accident have searched the early writings for the sources of his humor, his style, and his various characters, have combed his letters and notebooks for critical opinions, and have ransacked everything he wrote or read for indications of his literary taste. The investigation has turned up much about Samuel L. Clemens, the man, but surprisingly little about Mark Twain, the novelist.

Part of the difficulty is that most of the critics have ignored or misinterpreted his literary burlesques. Of all the apprentice writing, these are the only pieces which involve him directly in problems of plot and characterization, yet they have received little attention. The reasons for such neglect are not hard to find. First is the notion that burlesque is an inferior art form unworthy of serious or extended treatment. Second is the dominant tendency in criticism to view the burlesques merely as an elementary stage of Mark Twain's "realism."

That burlesque is an inferior genre is a necessary inference from the tenet that comedy is inferior to tragedy, a doctrine stemming ultimately from Aristotle, who regarded comedy as undignified and of minor value in comparison with the tragic or heroic poem. Albert Bigelow Paine's comments on Twain's use of burlesque in his books are prompted by a similar contrast between high and low. When he speaks of Livy's attempts to guide her husband's taste, he says, "A literary imp was always lying in wait for Mark Twain, the imp of the burlesque, tempting him to do the *outré,* the outlandish, the shocking thing. It was this that Olivia Clemens had to labour hardest against."[1] That this "literary imp" is a low creature becomes apparent when Paine discusses specific books. Of *The Innocents Abroad* he says:

The world has a weakness for its illusions: the splendor that falls on castle walls, the glory of the hills at evening, the pathos of the days that are no more. It answers to tenderness, even on the page of humor, and to genuine enthusiasm, sharply sensing the lack of these things; instinctively resenting, even when most amused by it, extravagance and burlesque.[2]

Burlesque, according to Paine, is inimical to splendor, glory, pathos, tenderness, and genuine enthusiasm. Behind his statement is an assumption about the relative positions of burlesque and other literary types which becomes almost explicit in his discussion of *A Connecticut Yankee.* In a passage reminiscent of many an older one deploring the mixture of comedy and tragedy in Elizabethan drama, he contrasts the high seriousness of some scenes with the low burlesque of others, declaring that the book's "greater appeal is marred almost to ruin by coarse and extravagant burlesque, which destroys illusion and antagonizes the reader often at the very moment when the tale should fill him with a holy fire of a righteous wrath against wrong."[3]

Miss Bellamy falls into the same error. She sets out with the commendable purpose of proving that Mark Twain was "much more the conscious craftsman than is generally believed." It soon appears, however, that craftsmanship in burlesque is the lower of two levels of ability. To open her discussion of Twain's burlesques, she asserts that "burlesque itself is neither easy nor simple" and declares that "Mark Twain was an artist in burlesque."[4] But these two statements must be measured against another in which Miss Bellamy speaks of Twain as a reformer:

> Mark Twain's strong impatience—with mankind, with the existing plan of things, with almost everything—was one factor which determined his use of burlesque as a vehicle of reform.... All of this was at the expense of the potential artist within him, forced to yield to the get-results-quick schemes of the humorist-reformer.[5]

In other words, craftsmanship in burlesque is a short cut which precludes development in some other sort of craftsmanship presumably of a higher order. The fallacy involved in such thinking about burlesque is obvious; both Paine and Bellamy confuse technical skill and attitude. It is clearly impossible to demonstrate that the writer of the perfect tragedy is more of a craftsman than the writer of the perfect burlesque.

The same failure to distinguish between skill and attitude is the root of the tendency to consider Twain's burlesques an elementary stage of realism. Edgar M. Branch illustrates the confusion. For him the term *realism* has several meanings, none indicated clearly, but in his discussion of burlesque, the word apparently is synonymous with *criticism,* for, according to Branch, a realist is, of necessity, a reformer. His interpretation of Twain's burlesques as "a corrective of insincerity and an antidote to decadent romance and practical abuse" leads him to assert that "[Twain's] burlesques place him among the realists and show that in practical affairs he was potentially a reformer." The statement not only equates *realist* with *reformer* but also establishes a hierarchy of realisms in which burlesque occupies a relatively low plane, for the burlesques serve to indicate only a potential reformer. Indeed, Branch declares that the burlesques "are not central to Mark Twain's genius"; they only "indicate certain lines of development." The assumption that burlesque is a basic tool of the realist-reformer leads to the inference that failure to criticize in a burlesque is the equivalent of technical inferiority. The realization that Twain combines criticism and comedy in his burlesques and that "of these the more important to him was comedy" causes Branch to conclude, "This fact makes his burlesques today seem inferior in technical ability and genuine humor."[6]

A large portion of the prevalent confusion about the relationships among burlesque, realism, and the reformer comes from Vernon L. Parrington's *Main Currents in American Thought*. In tracing Mark Twain's development from writer of burlesque to realist-reformer, Parrington makes a wide circuit which starts with frontier humor:

That Mark Twain should have begun by burlesquing life was itself a broad sign of his frontier origins. Since the first crossing of the Allegheny Mountains a swaggering extravagance of speech had been a hallmark of the Westerner. In part this swagger was an unconscious defense-mechanism against the drabness of frontier life; and in part it was the spontaneous expression of new experiences in an untrammeled world, the spirit of wilderness-leveling.

Because such humor is a "swaggering extravagance" cultivated in some measure to hide the "drabness of frontier life," one purpose then was to hide actuality or to obscure it so that it was unrecognizable, for, presumably, actuality was to the frontiersman what the Gorgons' glances were to Perseus. But almost immediately, frontier humor becomes realism: "This earliest backwoods humor had been done in realistic colors and bears the impress of authenticity." The reader must assume that a "swaggering extravagance" produces "realistic colors" and furthermore gives the "impress of authenticity."

The next step is even more bewildering: out of burlesque, one form of the extravagance which produces realistic color and authenticity, comes Mark Twain, the idealist.

It was this humor that Mark Twain inherited, and he enriched it with a wealth dug from his own large and generous nature. An incorrigible idealist, as all great humorists must be, he recreated some of the earlier types, translating Colonel Simon Suggs into Colonel Sellers, and Ransy Sniffle into Huck Finn.[7]

The identification of Twain as an idealist inevitably results in his transformation into a satirist; but the path from Mark Twain, satirist, to Mark Twain, reformer, theoretically easy and straight, is under Parrington's guidance more circuitous. Mark Twain, the reformer, comes not from the satirist-idealist but from the western humorist, a derivative of the older group of frontier humorists, now identified as "the old naturistic school." *Huckleberry Finn,* the supreme expression of the western philosophy imbibed from "the old naturistic school," is the triumph of Mark Twain, reformer and realist: "The rebel Huck is no other than the rebel Mark Twain whose wrath was quick to flame up against the unrighteous customs and laws of caste. If men were only honest realists—that is, if they were men and not credulous fools—how quickly the stables might be cleansed and life become decent and humane."[8] The logic takes another curious twist here: the reformer finally comes to rest firmly in the ranks of the realists, but the last clause seems to turn him toward the verges of idealism again.

Such concepts of burlesque are closely associated with the critical assumptions underlying the controversy between Van Wyck Brooks and Bernard DeVoto. Once again burlesque becomes involved in social criticism. Quoting Paine's remark about "the imp of the burlesque," and Olivia Clemens' hard labors against it, Brooks comments, "Well she laboured, and well Mark Twain laboured with her! It was the spirit of the artist, bent upon upsetting the whole apple-cart of bourgeois conventions."[9] Here "the imp of the burlesque" becomes "the spirit of the artist" which in turn becomes the reformer of or the revolutionist against "bourgeois conventions." But apparently *burlesque* does not always mean "the spirit of the artist" to Brooks, for he also cites this and other forms of humor as evidence of a compromise with the western environment. "So much for Mark Twain's motives in becoming a humorist," he writes.

> He had adopted this role unwillingly, as a compromise, at the expense of his artistic self-respect, because it afforded the only available means of satisfying that other instinct which, in the unconsciousness of his creative instinct, had become dominant in him, the gregarious, acquisitive instinct of the success-loving pioneer.[10]

Despite the contradictory concept of burlesque, Brooks still identifies the self-respecting artist with the social revolutionist. Burlesque, associated with reform, is not the spirit of rebellion but a compromise between it and conformity.

Bernard DeVoto is equally explicit on the subject, and equally confused. In his answer to Brooks he follows Parrington, connecting the frontier and western humor with realism: "In his analysis of Mark Twain, the eidolon 'Frontier' has a primary importance; yet Mr. Brooks fails to consider Frederick Jackson Turner's study of the frontier, the basis of realism in any discussion."[11] His next step gets to the heart of the matter:

> It is convenient to begin with the frontier humor characterized as anecdotal narrative. Its origin was the life at hand; its creators were the people who lived on the frontier, and, I have said, its overwhelming emphasis was on the folk themselves. In American literature, fantasy and realism exist side by side. In the same way, burlesque and extravaganza, which are theoretically derived from fantasy, are hardly to be separated from satire, a derivative of realism.[12]

His first two sentences seem to connect frontier humor with a reportorial treatment of actuality, but the remainder clearly connects realism with criticism if satire is to be a derivative of realism. Presumably, then, the frontier humorist, seeing life as it is, burlesques all in literature which departs from observed reality.

Such concepts of burlesque, no less than the assumption that burlesque is an inferior order of art, tend to minimize the technical skill requisite for burlesque and its importance in the training of the novelist. To treat burlesque as a manifestation of the realistic attitude necessarily, if realism is equated with social criticism, focuses attention not upon the craftsmanship but upon the writer's attitude toward his environment. In discussions of Twain's burlesques such an approach leads to the question of his reaction against, conformity to, or compromise with the society in which he lived, whether in the Mississippi Valley, Nevada, California, or Connecticut.

These critics apply the word *burlesque* more generally than to literary burlesque alone. To them, it includes burlesques of living people, oratory, and various types of writing as well as fiction; but that it also includes literary burlesque is clear when they discuss, for example, *The Innocents Abroad* as a burlesque of travel books or *Tom Sawyer* as a burlesque of Sunday-school literature. In analyzing Twain's literary burlesques, the critics all assume, as Branch does, that they were written as "a corrective of insincerity and an antidote to decadent romance," that is, as a criticism and refutation of the work or genre burlesqued. The assumption is the basis of DeVoto's coupling of burlesque and extravaganza, both dependent upon radical departures from observed reality, with realism, for in the passage quoted above he writes, "Burlesque and extravaganza, which are theoretically derived from fantasy, are hardly to be separated from satire, a derivative of realism." But even such a generally accepted concept of literary burlesque is open to question.

In the nineteenth-century American and British humor magazines, burlesques of Shakespeare and Boucicault, Jane Austen and Mrs. Braddon, Dickens and Ainsworth appear side by side. A critical faculty which reduces such a wide range of literary accomplishment to a single level of ridiculousness is difficult, if not impossible, to imagine. Furthermore, several writers have distinguished themselves in the very genre they have burlesqued. Thomas Dibdin, after writing *Bonifacio and Bridgetina; or The Knight of the Hermitage, or The Windmill Turett; or The Spectre of the North-East Gallery* (Covent Garden, 1808), one of the earliest burlesques of melodrama, wrote several successful melodramas. Douglas Jerrold, a founder of *Punch,* wrote a number of burlesques which appeared beside Thackeray's work in that magazine; but while he was doing so, he also wrote *Black-ey'd Susan,* frequently cited as the most typical Jolly-Jack-Tar type of melodrama. Mark Twain burlesqued the theme of the wandering heir's return, the basis of such a novel as *Ivanhoe,* with the Legend of Count Luigi in *The Innocents Abroad,* but seriously used the same plot device in *The Prince and the Pauper.* Such evidence suggests that a burlesque is not necessarily the result of a critical appraisal and condemnation of another work or literary device. It may reflect instead any one of a number of attitudes, such as an aversion for the particular book in question, a personal animus for an author, an innocuous desire to be funny, or, strange as it may seem, a desire to learn by imitation.

A statement in *Vanity Fair* (the house-organ, so to speak, of the New York Bohemians, the group of young writers who gathered in Pfaff's famous beer-cellar during the late 1850's and early 1860's, made literary burlesque their specialty, and lionized Walt Whitman) indicates that, to some of the Pfaffians at least, burlesque was nothing more than a frivolous game: "We are engaged in a noble work. We are doing for literature what the actors of the day are doing for the stage—we are simplifying matters—stripping them of their excrescences, and proving that everything is susceptible of being burlesqued."[13] The statement reveals a catholicity precluding critical discriminations.

Although Mark Twain's critics have assumed that literary burlesque necessarily springs from a critical attitude, such statements by nineteenth-century practitioners of the art indicate that to some of them the concept of criticism did not perforce enter into their definitions of the phrase. Instead, literary burlesque apparently meant merely a humorous imitation and exaggeration of the conventions in plot, characterization, or style peculiar to a literary type or a particular book, play, short story, or poem.[14]

If an aversion to the target work is not a necessary adjunct to the burlesque spirit, the writer might conceivably find the practice of burlesque a route to the construction of original works of fiction. This was the case with at least three English novelists—Fielding, Jane Austen, and Thackeray—all of whom followed the same path, advancing through three clearly distinguishable stages: burlesque, burlesque combined with original fiction, and finally independent construction. Thus Fielding's *Shamela* leads to *Joseph Andrews,* which in turn is followed by *Tom Jones.* Jane Austen went from unalloyed burlesque in *Love and Freindship* to the middle stage in *Northanger Abbey* and finally to independence in *Pride and Prejudice* and the other novels. Thackeray, of course, started with his various burlesques, including *Punch's Prize Novelists,* turned to the hybrid *Barry Lyndon,* and followed this with *Vanity Fair.* All of these writers, to some extent critical of the works they burlesqued, borrowed plot-devices from their targets for use in their own works and from their apprenticeship in burlesque learned skills later used in their novels. Jane Austen, for example, burlesqued the romantic elopement device of the sentimental novel in *Love and Freindship* but used the device herself in the Lydia-Wickham elopement of *Pride and Prejudice.* Thackeray turned his skill as a parodist to good account when he wrote *Henry Esmond* in the Addisonian style of the eighteenth century.

That either Fielding, Jane Austen, or Thackeray consciously set out to learn through burlesque the techniques of the novelists they attacked is doubtful, but one nineteenth-century American parodist states explicitly that learning from his "betters" was the motive for his sport. Bayard Taylor, one of the Pfaffian Bohemians, has left a record of what he calls in a prefatory remark "a good many random hours of thoughtless (or, at least, only half-thoughtful) recreation and amusement,—nothing else" in *The Echo Club and Other Literary Diversions.* In the guise of "The Ancient," he states the purpose behind his parodies:

And here, perhaps, is one result of our diversions, upon which we had not calculated, over and above the fun. I don't see why poets should not drill themselves in all that is technical, as well as painters, sculptors, opera-singers, or even orators. All the faculties called into play to produce rhythm, harmony of words, richness of the poetical dialect, choice of keys and cadences, may be made nimbler, more active, and more obedient to command, by even mechanical practice.[15]

All these considerations suggest the value of a study of Mark Twain's literary burlesques and their effect upon his later travel books and novels. Following an abortive attempt to write a burlesque of travel literature in the Thomas Jefferson Snodgrass letters of 1856, Twain passed through an apprenticeship in burlesque after his arrival in Virginia City, Nevada. In a period approximately delimited by the decade 1863 to 1873 he wrote, besides the early travel-burlesques, a number of smaller burlesques, many in the condensed form first used by Thackeray in *Punch's Prize Novelists*. Some of them, still unpublished, have received no critical attention. The purpose of this volume is to discover his debt to this apprenticeship in burlesque when he turned to independent construction.

Such a study will show that the period from 1855 to 1885 was one of experimentation during which Twain drew heavily upon his training in burlesque in an attempt to impose structure upon his fictive world. His problem was not new, but he encountered much more difficulty than most novelists in solving it, if indeed one can say he solved it completely. Adhering to Howells' concept of the novelist as a reporter of actuality, he could not easily reduce an apparently formless or chaotic reality to the coherence of a plot. From 1866 to 1885 he struggled with the problem of structure, in the process passing through the three stages of development which Fielding, Austen, and Thackeray had traversed before him. But in the third stage he failed to achieve a similar technical mastery of his materials. After the early Snodgrass letters, he adopted with almost no reservations the conventions of a currently popular type of travel-literature burlesque when he wrote the Sandwich Islands letters. Through a series of modifications and adaptations of the

conventions, he evolved a new type of travel narrative in *Roughing It.* His major efforts in *Tom Sawyer, The Prince and the Pauper,*
and *Huckleberry Finn* were expended first on transforming early
burlesques into skeletons for his novels and then on adapting the
structural achievements of the travel narratives to the craft of the
novel, achieving an almost complete realization of a new and distinctive structural pattern in *Huckleberry Finn.* Total technical
mastery was lacking, however, and in his next novel, *A Connecticut
Yankee,* he abandoned the pattern so painfully developed, retreated
to an earlier solution to the problem of structure in fiction, and
explored in a new direction. For this reason, the present discussion
will be limited to the works written between the beginning of his
career and 1885.

2

Apprenticeship in Burlesque

INTENT upon theses concerned with a reaction against or conformity to certain norms of social behavior, most of Twain's critics have tended to simplify the actual complexity of California and Nevada society in order to obtain a sharp contrast with the East, a contrast between a virile primitivism and an effete genteelism. Influenced perhaps by the disproportionately large amount of space devoted to the pocket-mining episode in *Roughing It,* these critics have made the miner's shack at Tuolumne a symbol of Mark Twain's western experiences, in the process minifying the importance of the much greater length of time spent in association with practicing writers in the offices of a large metropolitan literary weekly, the San Francisco *Golden Era.* The West symbolized by the miner's cabin furnished Twain with much material for his later books, but the literary associations formed in San Francisco had a lasting effect upon his craftsmanship. An immediate result of the San Francisco years was the combination of literary taste and techniques reflected in the large number of burlesques written during the late sixties and early seventies. A more distant but no less direct result was the development of the structural patterns not only of his greatest travel narratives but also of *Tom Sawyer, The Prince and the Pauper,* and *Huckleberry Finn.*

When Samuel L. Clemens joined the staff of the *Enterprise* in 1862, he touched the periphery of an intellectual environment entirely new to him, a literary circle. A year and nine months later, he moved into the center of the circle by joining Ada Clare, Bret

Harte, Charles Henry Webb, and other Bohemians in San Francisco. Prior to 1862, his social and intellectual contacts were only indirectly significant for the development of the writer. He read novels of the period, especially the works of Dickens, laughed at the jokes of contemporary humorists, talked with others who had read much the same material, and set a great number of words in type. From such contacts came little of use to him later in solving his own problems as a writer. To be sure, his reading and conversations led him to such early endeavors as "The Dandy Frightening the Squatter" and the Thomas Jefferson Snodgrass letters, but the contrast in concept and quality between these and the later works proves that his activities affected but slightly the later Mark Twain. Before Samuel L. Clemens could become Mark Twain, he needed close association with other writers. Virginia City and San Francisco supplied the need; his earlier life had not.

After examining minutely the culture of Hannibal, Dixon Wecter concluded, "The real Hannibal was neither the total cultural desert imagined by Van Wyck Brooks in *The Ordeal of Mark Twain* nor the seat of the muses patriotically conceived by Minnie Brashear in *Mark Twain, Son of Missouri*.... The basic culture of Sam Clemens' Hannibal was literate but not literary."[1] Twain's immediate intellectual environments during the four years as a tramp printer must be characterized in much the same fashion: literate but not literary. In New York, Philadelphia, Muscatine, Keokuk, and Cincinnati he worked long hours with other printers and found time, in New York especially, to read books borrowed from libraries. True, in these years he set a great deal of written matter into type, but little of such material can be classified as literature. Furthermore, the process of hand typesetting is not conducive to a critical reading of long texts.

In Nevada and California, however, the young journalist worked and talked with writers, some of whom had a fairly wide reputation: Ada Clare, the famous or, to some, the infamous "Queen of the Bohemians," Charles Henry Webb, Orpheus C. Kerr, Artemus

Ward, and Adah Isaacs Menken, all from the now scattered group of New York Bohemians. Locally well known were Dan DeQuille, Joe Lawrence, Bret Harte, Prentice Mulford, Charles W. Stoddard, and Ina Coolbrith. Through such associations and his connection with the *Golden Era,* Twain made his first extended acquaintance with the dominant form of nineteenth-century British and American humor, the burlesque novel, and with a type of travel-burlesque then enjoying a widespread popularity. Prior to his arrival in Nevada, he had undoubtedly read both burlesque novels and travel-burlesques in humor magazines. During his years as a tramp printer, he probably had set a number of burlesque novels into type: because of their brevity, they were frequently reprinted in the newspapers. But among his associates in Nevada and California were well-known writers who had written such burlesques and who could guide him in his attempts to write similar pieces.

By the middle of the nineteenth century, the burlesque novel had acquired a fairly conventional character in the hands of English and American humorists through the constant use of the burlesque devices employed by Fielding in *Shamela* (1741), the first English burlesque novel. The title of the burlesque is usually a humorous play upon that of the original: "Lady Dawdley's Secret" for *Lady Audley's Secret,* "Chikken Hazzard" for *Foul Play,* or "The Missouri Rabbles" for *Les Miserables.* The burlesque imitates the original not only in title but in extended subtitle if the original had one, list of other works by the same author, prefatory remarks, and appropriate verse parodies at the head of each chapter. But unlike *Shamela,* which is nearly 23,000 words in length, the typical nineteenth-century burlesque novel ranges between 500 and 2,500 words, with chapters varying between 50 and 500. The extreme condensation, appearing first in *Punch's Prize Novelists* (later collected and printed as *Novels by Eminent Hands*), was Thackeray's contribution to the conventions of the genre. Abandoning the extended length of the earlier burlesque, he reduced his to a size easily accommodated in the pages of a periodical, thus making possible the great popularity of the burlesque novel in the nineteenth century. He was copied by a host of others not only in *Punch* but in the other English comic magazines, such as *Fun, Judy,* and *Punch and Judy,* and in such American imitations as *Yankee Notions* and *Vanity Fair.*[2]

Several of the Bohemians with whom Twain associated during his western years were well practiced in the art of the burlesque novel. Artemus Ward had contributed a substantial number to *Vanity Fair,* principally during his editorship of that magazine in 1862 and 1863. Orpheus C. Kerr, too, had written burlesque novels for *Vanity Fair,* although by the time he arrived in San Francisco in 1863 he had abandoned the writing of burlesques for the more congenial task of writing political lampoons.[3] But the two men most active in the field of burlesque and most important in influence exerted upon Twain were Bret Harte and Charles Henry Webb.

The story of Bret Harte's career as a San Francisco Bohemian is well known and needs no extended rehearsal. It suffices to note that he was the American whose skill in writing burlesque novels rivaled Thackeray's. In January, 1861, he began a series of burlesque novels that ran sporadically under the pseudonym "J. Keyser" in the *Golden Era* until March 1, 1863. Most of these burlesques are trivial, but toward the end of the series at least three show a development of skill in parody as well as in burlesque: "Victor Hugo's New Gospel, 'Les Miserables' *Fantine"* (August 3, 1862); *"La Femme* from the French of M. Michelet" (September 14, 1862); and "More Miserables, A Saturated Romance in Five Portions by Victim Howgo" (January 4 to February 1, 1863). These show clear indications of the skill characteristic of the *Condensed Novels* written for the *Californian.* The *Condensed Novels* themselves (New York: Carleton, 1867) were immediately recognized in both the United States and England as the high point of the burlesque-novel movement.

Charles Henry Webb, a New York Bohemian who migrated to California with Kerr, Ada Clare, and the others of his group, had been a frequent contributor to and a staunch supporter of *Vanity Fair* during the editorship of Artemus Ward. While in California he wrote two burlesque novels later published in the East: *Liffith Lank; or Lunacy* (New York: Carleton, 1866), a burlesque of Reade's *Griffith Gaunt; or, Jealousy,* and *St. Twel'mo; or, the Cuneiform Cyclopedist of Chattanooga* (New York: Carleton, 1867), a burlesque of Augusta Jane Evans' *St. Elmo.* These and his rather extensive list of burlesques and parodies in verse were collected and published in 1876 as *Parodies, Prose and Verse.* In addition he wrote one of the most popular stage burlesques produced in San Francisco in the period, *Arrah-no-Poke,* a burlesque of Boucicault's melodrama *Arrah-no-Poque.*

Twain quickly adapted himself to this group. It is true that his first explicit claim to the title of Bohemian occurs in a letter to Charles Coolbrith dated April 23, 1867: "How is Bret? He is publishing with a Son of a Bitch who will swindle him, & he may print that opinion if he chooses, with my name signed to it. I don't know how his book is coming on—we of Bohemia keep away from Carleton."[4] But before this, other writers in the California and Nevada papers recognized him as a Bohemian. For example, Twain's rival, Albert S. Evans, San Francisco correspondent for the Gold Hill *News,* calls him a "sage-brush Bohemian" in a letter printed in the *News,* January 29, 1866.[5]

Contact with the self-consciously sophisticated Bohemians caused Mark Twain not only to adopt the title of Bohemian but also to alter his ideas about his writing. For a time he became disdainful of his humorous sketches in the frontier mode. In a letter written January 20, 1866, he is quite explicit about his attitude:

To think that, after writing many an article a man might be excused for thinking tolerably good, those New York people should single out a villainous backwoods sketch to compliment me on!—"Jim Smiley and His Jumping Frog"—a squib which would never have been written but to please Artemus Ward, and then it reached New York too late to appear in his book.[6]

The phrase "villainous backwoods sketch" is important as it reveals an orientation toward the sophistication affected by his San Francisco associates. Under the tutelage of the Bohemians, he had cultivated an urbane attitude and style, imitating his friends in an attempt to impress the audience to which they had directed their efforts. But ironically, that audience had chosen to ignore all this and to celebrate a sketch of exactly the opposite character.[7]

Of course, the most obvious, although probably the least reliable, indication that Twain had cast his lot with the Bohemians of San Francisco is his adoption of the burlesque-novel form, the appearance of which in his writings is coincident with his assumption of the Bohemian name and attitude. If the period of his Bohemian apprenticeship is defined as the years between 1863, when his first condensed burlesque appeared, and 1871, when he had conquered his Bohemian sophistication sufficiently to recognize merit in the "Jumping Frog" story, the greater part of his apprenticeship was one in the writing of burlesque. Nearly half of the fifty-one short items written in this period, twenty-three to be exact, are either fully realized literary burlesques or anecdotes and sketches depending primarily upon burlesque and parody for their humor. The range of this material is wide: from "Lucretia Smith's Soldier," a condensed burlesque of Civil War romances, to "A Visit to Niagara," which includes some excellent parodies of Cooper.

Although he wrote condensed burlesques of both novels and plays, the burlesque novels predominate. Only three of his pieces concern the drama: "Ingomar the Barbarian" (1863); "The Killing of Julius Caesar Localized" (1864), which follows Shakespeare's play but uses the form of a newspaper column; and "Burlesque Il Trovatore" (1866), unpublished.[8] There are seven condensed novels: "Lucretia Smith's Soldier" (1864); "The Story of the Bad Little Boy" (1865); "Who Was He?" (1867), an unfinished and unpublished burlesque of Hugo's *Les Travailleurs de la mer;*[9] "The Story of Mamie Grant, the Child-Missionary" (1868), unpublished;[10] "Burlesque *L'Homme Qui Rit*" (c. 1869), unpublished;

"The Boy's Manuscript" (c. 1870); and "The Story of the Good Little Boy" (1870). Three, although obviously condensed burlesques, do not exhibit the characteristic division into miniature chapters. They are "The Story of the Bad Little Boy," "The Boy's Manuscript," and "The Story of the Good Little Boy."

Part of Twain's tutelage during his Bohemian apprenticeship came from Bret Harte, whose role Twain acknowledged in the often quoted letter to Aldrich written in 1871:

But I did hate to be accused of plagiarizing Bret Harte, who trimmed and trained and schooled me patiently until he changed me from an awkward utterer of coarse grotesquenesses to a writer of paragraphs and chapters that have found a certain favor in the eyes of some of the very decentest people in the land.[11]

Whether or not Twain's schooling included training in burlesque would be difficult to say, although presumably Harte's use of the condensed-novel form induced Twain to experiment in the same genre. Other than this presumption and the statement in the Aldrich letter, no evidence indicates clearly that Harte was Twain's guide in burlesque techniques.

On the other hand, sufficiently tangible evidence suggests that Twain owed a substantial debt to Charles Henry Webb as a tutor in burlesque—a debt never explicitly acknowledged, but one showing clearly enough in several burlesque devices borrowed from Webb. The association with Webb was as close as that with Harte, if not closer. In as much as Webb was the founder of the *Californian*, Twain, as contributor, came into as much contact with him as with Harte. Furthermore, Webb published Twain's first book, an act Twain appreciated greatly at the time despite his later denunciations of Webb's dealings with him in this matter. But the relationship extended further. The two men were close enough to joke publicly at each other's expense with impunity. In his letter to the *Enterprise* dated February 25, 1866, Twain felt free to deal humorously with Webb, a compliment he never paid Harte.[12] Webb returned the honor at least twice, with a reference to "The Jumping Frog" and a mention of Mark Twain in *St. Twel'mo* and with a humorous parable of Twain's role in the Sanitary Flour Sack affair in *John Paul's Book*.[13] In *Roughing It* Twain retaliated by characterizing Webb as the "dissolute stranger" who spoiled the serialized novel in the *Weekly Occidental*. The friendship, deeper than the relationship of editor and contributor, probably had its basis in an association formed while the two were fellow drama critics, Twain for the San Francisco *Dramatic Chronicle* and Webb for the *Bulletin*. Quite possibly the two made the rounds of the playhouses together; certainly they met frequently during those rounds.

Like the other nineteenth-century writers of burlesque, Webb leaned heavily upon the pun and the literal interpretation of metaphors, but his elaborately artificial style when he is not actually parodying that of his model is more distinctive. Alliterative and rhythmic, it frequently includes assonances and rhymes as well:

It was a gallant chase, and our dreamy virgin's back got up. Her golden hair streamed and her gray eyes watered, as lithe and blithe she sat upon her great white gelding, riding over huntsmen as well as hounds, and jumping ditches and hedges where the stoutest steeple-chase riders of the country were stuck and staked.

Such stylistic devices appear in the work of no other San Francisco writer at this time with the exception of Harte's *Muck a Muck*. Harte, however, indebted to Webb's stage burlesque *Arrah-no-Poke*, acknowledges his source in Genevra's song:

O *Arrah, ma dheelish,* the distant *dudheen*
Lies soft in the moonlight, *ma bouchal vourneen:*
The springing *gossoons* on the heather are still
And the *caubeens* and *colleens* are heard on the hills.

The malapropos Gaelic used by Harte copies another device Webb used often, but to best effect in *St. Twel'mo*—that is, the consciously inappropriate use of grandiose terms and foreign expressions:

"Aged grandsire," replied the child, "to plunge *in medias res,* inaugurating my narration without an appogiatura; touching the origin of the infusoria, Leuwenhoek, Gleichen, Zenzis-Khan, Alexander, Attila, Gurowski, to say nothing of the iridescent Illuminati of Boston, (this last was spoken sarcastically, for Etna was a true Southern girl,) all entertain different opinions. Also, in the course of my varied studies, I observe with regret that, as regards the Rhinoplastic or Taliacotian operation, as to whether the cellular tissue should be dissected down to the periosteum, leaving the *os humerus* or lumbar region to infringe upon the pericardium, to the disarrangement and displacement of the *arbor vitae,* chirurgeons differ, nor are they even united as to the best method of demephitization; ischuretics also are still a matter of dispute. And when chirurgeons who have passed beyond the stormy esophagus of science and gained the smooth Bahr-Sheitan beyond . . . differ by so much as a dodecatemorion, who shall decide? You may, *par example,* imagine that, because I am a woman, I have no right to express an opinion thus freely and *con amore;* but, is woman merely an adscriptus glebae chameleonlike—."[14]

During his years of close association with Webb, from 1864 to 1867, Twain began to use Webb's stylistic devices. Prior to this period, he had used the country-bumpkin style, in the Thomas Jefferson Snodgrass letters for example, with the usual trappings: misspellings, lapses into rural or countrified metaphors and similes, and malapropisms. He had also demonstrated a skill in parody, although as yet he had not attempted parodies of literary models. For example, in his December 5, 1862, letter to the *Enterprise* he manages a fair parody of the committee-report style, and in an *Enterprise* letter a year later, December 5, 1863, he parodies the oratory of L. O. Stearns, one of the Nevada legislators.[15] His own style during the *Enterprise* days is clear and reportorial, generally free of conscious rhetorical devices.

The pieces written between 1864 and 1867 reveal the growth of a new consciousness in his use of language. More and more frequently alliterative sentences appear in his prose, such as one from "Aurelia's Unfortunate Young Man": "He was hurrying home with happiness in his heart, when he lost his hair forever." The sentence also illustrates another new development, the tendency to finish such alliterative passages with a marked rhythm, in this case with the definitely rhythmical "when he lost his hair forever." A shorter but similar example appears in "The Killing of Julius Caesar 'Localized'": "He takes a living delight in this labor of love." The phrase "living delight" is meaningless, if examined logically; the only possible explanation for it in the prose of a man normally remarkable for his clarity is the conscious desire to gain additional alliteration and a more marked rhythm with the insertion of the word "living." When he created a burlesque role for himself in the Sandwich Islands letters, that of a sophisticated traveler, he used this alliterative and rhythmic style as an indication of his sophistication.[16]

Webb's second distinctive device, the consciously inappropriate use of technical terms and foreign expressions, first appears in Twain's prose in the fashion sketch "The Pioneer Ball," written for the *Enterprise* in November, 1865:

Mrs. W. M. was attired in an elegant pâté de foie gras, made expressly for her, and was greatly admired. Miss S. had her hair done up. She was the center of attraction for the gentlemen and the envy of all the ladies. Mrs. G. W. was tastefully dressed in a *tout ensemble,* and was greeted with deafening applause wherever she went.

In time the use of this device became a fine art with Twain. In the Sandwich Islands letters his performance with seafaring terms is rather juvenile:

"Let go the main-hatch. Belay! Haul away on your tops'l jib! Belay! Clew up your top-gallants'l spanker-boom halliards! Belay! Port your gaff-tops'l sky-scrapers! Belay! Lively, you lubbers! Take a reef in the lee scuppers! Belay! Mr. Baxter, it's coming on to blow at about four bells in the hog-watch; have everything taut and trim for it. Belay!"

But soon he gained sufficient skill to use the device successfully as the basis for his characterization of the "Oracle" in *The Innocents Abroad.* This man, like Etna in Webb's burlesque, uses erudite words with a supreme disregard for their fitness in the context and when challenged on the score of his erudition, invents authorities to support himself. Remarking upon the Pillars of Hercules, he says:

"Do you see that there hill out there on that African coast? It's one of them Pillows of Herkewls, I should say—and there's the ultimate one alongside of it."

"The ultimate one—that is a good word—but the Pillars are not both on the same side of the strait." (I saw he had been deceived by a carelessly written sentence in the Guide Book.)

"Well, it ain't for you to say, nor for me. Some authors states it that way, and some states it different. Old Gibbons don't say nothing about it,—just shirks it complete—Gibbons always done that when he got stuck—but there is Rolampton, what does *he* say? Why, he says that they was both on the same side, and Trinculian, and Sobaster, and Syraccus, and Langomarganbl—"

Years later, the combination of these two devices produced that masterpiece of burlesque prose in "A Double-Barreled Detective Story":

It was a crisp and spicy morning in early October. The lilacs and laburnums, lit with the glory-fires of autumn, hung burning and flashing in the upper air, a fairy bridge provided by kind Nature for the wingless wild things that have their homes in the tree-tops and would visit together; the larch and the pomegranate flung their purple and yellow flames in brilliant broad splashes along the slanting sweep of the woodland; the sensuous fragrance of innumerable deciduous flowers rose upon the swooning atmosphere; far in the empty sky a solitary oesophagus slept upon motionless wing; everywhere brooded stillness, serenity, and the peace of God.

"Oesophagus" is a relatively rare word, particularly in such a context; certainly more than mere accident produces the echo of Webb's burlesque passage written in 1867 in *St. Twel'mo*: "And when chirurgeons who have passed beyond the stormy esophagus of science and gained the smooth Bahr-Sheitan beyond..." The echo shows that Twain learned his lesson from Webb, and learned it well.

As a result of his recent recruitment into the ranks of the Bohemians, the Clemens who boarded the steamer *Ajax* on March 7, 1866, headed for the Sandwich Islands, was equipped with a new urbanity and a new consciousness of rhythmic and alliterative effects in language and of tricks to be played with words. At this time he probably also conceived of burlesque, not as a corrective of decadent romance, but merely as a form of literary fun. Twain himself has left no statement indicating clearly his conception of burlesque in his Bohemian days, but an implication that he shared the Bohemian belief, suggested by the declaration in *Vanity Fair* quoted earlier, that burlesque is nothing but innocuous sport, appears in a letter written by Joseph Goodman, Twain's editor on the *Territorial Enterprise* and his lifelong friend. The letter, written in 1883, concerns a burlesque *Hamlet* on which the two were working:

I was speaking to Barrett once about your idea, and he thought it would be a sort of sacrilege. That might be the opinion also of the goody-goodies who are howling about the "Passion Play" (the most impressive presentation of Christianity ever witnessed); but you and I know such talk is all fudge. Anything is legitimate sport and game— and especially Shakespeare, who cribbed right and left, and ridiculed nearly everybody and everything by turns.[17]

Twain's friendship with Webb and the other San Francisco Bohemians, his adoption of the Bohemian pose of sophistication, and his stylistic borrowings from Webb argue strongly for the assumption that the attitude indicated by Goodman's letter of 1883 was gained in San Francisco in the middle sixties. Presumably, therefore, as Twain boarded the *Ajax* he felt no constraint upon him which would prevent the use in his own writing of devices and situations previously burlesqued, or indeed which would restrain him from borrowing directly from his burlesques in the construction of original works of fiction. The assumption and presumption are borne out by the record of his subsequent development as a writer.

3

The Travel Books: Narrative-Plank and Narrator

MARK TWAIN'S first important achievements in form came not in the novel but in the travel narrative. Using as the basis of his experiments ingredients borrowed from a currently popular type of travel-literature burlesque, Twain evolved three major and distinctive structural devices.

The most elemental of the three is the simple alternation of humorous and serious episodes, a device Twain describes in his letter to Livy dated November 28, 1871:

Livy darling, good house, but they laughed too much.—A great fault with the lecture is that I have no way of turning it into a serious & instructive vein at will. *Any* lecture of mine ought to be a running narrative-plank, with square holes in it, six inches apart, all the length of it, & then in my mental shop I ought to have plugs (half marked "serious" & the other marked "humorous") to select from & jam into these holes according to the temper of the audience.[1]

By 1871, however, he had already achieved a greater measure of unity in each humorous-serious pair by making the second episode of the pair not only a tonal contrast but a complementary comment upon the same subject, the very contrast in tone expressing an implicit judgment upon the first episode. In a letter to Mrs. Fairbanks dated March 6, 1879, he describes the device while discussing the intended use of "The Great French Duel" (Chapter VII) in *A Tramp Abroad*:

I shall use that chapter in the book—it will follow a perfectly serious

26

description of 5 very bloody student-duels which I witnessed in Heidelberg one day—a description which simply describes the terrific spectacle, with no jests interlarded & no comments added. The contrast between that chapter and the next one (the Gambetta duel) will be the silent but eloquent comment.[2]

To furnish the narrative-plank for such serious-humorous contrasts, Twain borrowed two distinctive characters from the contemporary travel-literature burlesques and made them his second important structural device: a character-axis formed by the companionship of a sophisticated and sentimental gentleman and an unregenerate and insensitive associate. By apportioning the serious and pseudo-serious material to the gentleman and the comic to the unregenerate companion, Twain formed the character-axis into a fictive frame unifying the various serious-comic contrasts into a conflict of personalities and opinions.

The third and most important structural device is actually a combination and modification of the first two: a narrator who, unsophisticated and unregenerate at the moment of narration, was, however, sophisticated and sentimental at the outset of the adventures to be narrated. The narrative itself, the record of the transforming experiences, consists of a series of contrasts between the expectations of the inexperienced narrator (actually burlesques of the literature forming the expectations) and the disillusioning actuality.

The development of these three structural devices began in the 1866 Sandwich Islands letters, continued in *The Innocents Abroad,* and terminated in *Roughing It* with the creation of a new genre neither travel narrative nor burlesque of travel literature, although it includes much burlesque. Twain's structural experiments in the travel narrative ceased with the achievement of *Roughing It,* but both *A Tramp Abroad* and *Life on the Mississippi* attest that the formal principles of the earlier narratives had become habitual modes of composition.

I

Exactly how or when Twain became acquainted with the travel-burlesque elements basic to his structural experiments must remain a matter of conjecture. Presumably the acquaintance was made in San Francisco during Twain's association with the Bohemians, for the ingredients of his later structural patterns appeared only toward the end of his sojourn in San Francisco. Whether he gained his knowledge independently by studying travel-burlesque in contemporary humor magazines or dependently under the tutorship of the Bohemians is problematical, but certainly sometime between 1856 and 1866 he altered his concept of travel-burlesque to conform with a pattern popular among the Bohemians.

A contrast between the Thomas Jefferson Snodgrass letters and the Sandwich Islands letters readily reveals the new burlesque pattern he had acquired. The two sets of correspondence are ideal for the purpose: each is a series of letters based on an actual journey, in each Twain imposes a fiction upon the actual events, and in each Twain creates a fictive narrator who uses the first person pronoun but who, nevertheless, is clearly distinguishable from the author, Mark Twain. But they were written ten years apart, the Snodgrass letters in 1856, the Sandwich Island letters in 1866.

The major difference is the narrator in each. In the earlier set, Twain poses as Thomas Jefferson Snodgrass, a simple country bumpkin. In the first letter, Snodgrass displays an amazing lack of sophistication, the author unskilfully betraying his intention in Snodgrass' use of the word *unsophisticated* to characterize himself: "Finally Mr. Cesar hisself come in with a crown on, folks called it, but it looked to my unsofisticated vision like a hat without any crown about it."[3] Totally ignorant of such urban pastimes as play-going and such modern machines as the "iron horse," he reminds the reader of Jonathan in Tyler's *The Contrast*. In fact, Snodgrass is well within the Jonathan tradition of humor. Although he recognizes his lack of sophistication, he is still firmly convinced of the importance not only of himself but also of his home town, "the general starting pint of the inhabitants of North America." Keokuk, a name to conjure with, the *ne plus ultra* for all his comparisons, is the magic charm he uses to overawe the policeman who removes him from the theater after the first disturbance: "He took me out and after I explained to him how St. Louis would fizzle out if Keokuk got offended at her, he let me go back, makin me promise not to make any more music durin the evening."

But despite his chauvinistic pride in Keokuk and its environs, he almost immediately recognizes that his adventures in the big city and on his travels set him apart from the stay-at-homes in Keokuk. By virtue of his experiences, he has become the world traveler, the cultured man of the world, whose language tends to be beyond the comprehension of those who have not seen and learned so much. When his language becomes too erudite in the opening paragraph of the third letter, he must translate: "It mought be that some people think your umble sarvent has 'shuffled off this mortal quile' and bid an eternal adoo to this subloonary atmosphere—narry time. He aint dead, but sleepeth. That expreshun are figerative, and go to signerfy that he's pooty much quit scribblin."

Evidence that Twain was attempting a burlesque of the travel narrative as a genre appears twice in the series. At the beginning of the second letter Snodgrass explicitly states a travel book is in the offing:

You know arter going down there to St. Louis, and seein so many wonderful things, I wanted to see more—so I took a notion to go a travelin, so as to see the world, and then write a book about it—a kind o daily journal like—and have all in gold on the back of it, "Snodgrass' Dierrea," or somethin of that kind, like other authors that visits forren parts.

Toward the end of the same letter, he refers once again to the notion and to what is considered fashionable in such books. But the series can hardly be called a burlesque of travel literature. Despite the explicit statements about travel books and the coarse pun reflecting upon the effusions found therein, little if any of the reader's laughter centers upon the conventions of travel literature. Instead the laughter focuses upon Snodgrass, not because he embodies attitudes and performs activities recognizably typical of travelers who write books, but because he falls far short of such travelers. The difference in comic focus appears most clearly in Snodgrass' attempt at erudite diction. In a burlesque of travel books, the comedy arises, in part, from the author's fidelity to the essence of travel-book diction and from the reader's consciousness of a little too much cliché. In Twain's series, however, the comedy comes from Snodgrass' blunders, his unawareness of his deficiencies. The reader, noticing the misspellings, the solecisms, and the ignorance concerning the word *coil,* laughs at the difference between the aspiration and the execution.

II

The Sandwich Islands letters represent a notable advance in burlesque technique, an advance best illustrated in the characterization of the narrator, Mr. Twain.[4] Mr. Twain is quite capable of improving upon any traveler not only in travel but also in the art of writing travel literature. His refinement is such a marked characteristic that he expects some of it at least to penetrate his irresponsible companion, Brown. Of course, he is disappointed in the expectation, never more so than when Brown tries to collect the Cook memorial as a souvenir: "Why, Brown, I am surprised at you —and hurt. I am grieved to think that a man who has lived so long in the atmosphere of refinement which surrounds me can be guilty of such vandalism as this." Furthermore, he is a sentimentalist to the extent that he cannot pity Brown, "this bitter enemy to sentiment," when Brown becomes seasick and needs an application of poetry as an emetic. In addition to his refinement and sentimentality, Mr. Twain is socially proper and considerate; he must not only upbraid Brown for frequent breaches in etiquette but also reprimand him for his "inconsiderate levity" when Brown nicknames the bullock

"Captain Gordon" because, like the Captain, the bullock "lays down so much." Finally, Mr. Twain is a man of sensibility whose soul is so stirred by picturesque scenery that he must apostrophize. During the moonlight ride on the steed Oahu, he is impressed "by the profound silence and repose that rested over the beautiful landscape" to the extent that he cannot hold his tongue. Like Mr. Yorick, he must either speak or weep. Mr. Twain speaks:

"What a picture is here slumbering in the solemn glory of the moon! How strong the rugged outlines of the dead volcano stand out against the clear sky! What a snowy fringe marks the bursting of the surf over the long, curved reef! How calmly the dim city sleeps yonder in the plain! How soft the shadows lie upon the stately mountains that border the dream-haunted Manoa Valley! What a grand pyramid of billowy clouds towers above the storied Pari! How the grim warriors of the past seem flocking in ghostly squadrons to their ancient battlefield again—how the wails of the dying well up from the—"[5]

"The horse called Oahu," apparently overcome by the outburst of rhetoric, interrupts him at this point by sitting down.

Weak in many respects, the series of letters, as a whole, is not a first-class burlesque, but Mr. Twain's apostrophe illustrates the writer's advance in skill during the ten years since the Snodgrass letters. The apostrophe provokes laughter not because Mr. Twain is incompetent in his chosen task but because he is much too competent. The accumulation of typical travel-book clichés overwhelms the reader as completely as it does the horse Oahu. The strength of the burlesque comes from the fact that the language is completely suited to the character and the character is a humorously distorted but nevertheless a fairly accurate reflection of the traveler who writes books.

Twain's new skill springs from an acquaintance with a well-established type of nineteenth-century English and American travel-burlesque, an acquaintance gained possibly from his own reading in the humor magazines, more probably from a combination of such reading and the instruction of his Bohemian friends in San Francisco.

The type derives from William Combe's three tours of Dr. Syntax: *Dr. Syntax in Search of the Picturesque* (1809), *The Second Tour of Dr. Syntax in Search of Consolation* (1820), and *The Third Tour of Dr. Syntax in Search of a Wife* (1821).[6]

Travel-burlesques were, of course, not new to English literature when Combe wrote the first tour for the *Poetical Magazine* in 1809. Swift's *Gulliver's Travels* is, on one level, a burlesque of travel literature. But, according to Combe, the Syntax series owed less to previous travel-burlesques than it did to the mock-heroic tradition; in Canto XII of the first tour he writes,

> You'll see, at once, in this Divine,
> Quixote and Parson Adams shine:
> An hero well combin'd you'll view
> For FIELDING and CERVANTES too.[7]

The structure of the Dr. Syntax poems is obviously a derivative of the knight-errant tradition on which *Don Quixote* is built. Yet very little of the mock-heroic actually appears in the series. Indeed an important difference between Don Quixote and Dr. Syntax connects the traveler of the relevant nineteenth-century travel-burlesques with Dr. Syntax, not with Don Quixote. The deranged Knight of La Mancha knows no reality except that derived from his reading in the romances. Anyone purporting to see another reality is obviously a victim of enchantment. Sancho Panza, blinded by magic spells, may claim to see windmills, but Don Quixote sees giants. Dr. Syntax and the burlesque travelers who follow him are not so deluded. With them the question is a choice not between two realities but between two halves of a single reality. Dr. Syntax chooses for reasons of taste to ignore some aspects of what he sees and to concentrate on others, by this process eliminating the blemishes of the natural scene and producing the picturesque:

> What man of taste my right will doubt,
> To put things in, or leave them out?

> 'Tis more than right, it is a duty,
> If we consider landscape beauty:
> He ne'er will as an artist shine,
> Who copies Nature line by line.[8]

Although Syntax resembles Parson Adams and Quixote to a small extent, he is actually much closer to Mr. Yorick of Sterne's *Sentimental Journey*. Like Yorick, he is sentimental to the extreme, especially given to soliloquies upon picturesque and melancholy scenes, as, for example, his apostrophe upon the churchyard in Canto VIII of the first tour.

The good doctor's pretense to refinement and sentiment provided one convention in a large group of subsequent nineteenth-century travel-burlesques. His activities furnished two others. Impelled by interests both artistic and scientific, he searched for picturesque scenes to be drawn in his sketchbook and for "something curious" to copy into his notebook. A large number of "travelers" in later nineteenth-century travel-burlesques are either actual artists or of an artistic bent; those who are not are "scientific" observers of man and nature, and not a few are both.

The subsequent development of the Syntax type of travel-burlesque produced another well-defined convention, the ebullient traveling companion, a vernacular character whose lack of reverence for the picturesque and for the social niceties frequently causes the refined traveler much misery. The origin of this companion is lost in shadows, but probably he descends from Sancho Panza. Although the word *companion* serves to identify the convention, the character actually appears in a variety of shapes: sometimes he is a servant whose relationship with the traveler is marked by a familiarity exceeding the normal servant-master relationship; sometimes he is a guide, employed during the course of the journey, whose familiarity with the traveler is similar to that of the servant; sometimes he is a fellow-traveler equal in social status to the narrator but inferior in refinement, a young man attached to the cultivated traveler either through the efforts of a parent or friend or through the persuasion of the cultivated traveler himself in hopes of refining his manners and improving his tastes. His principal function, however, is similar to Sancho's. Just as Sancho serves to keep before the reader the actuality which the deluded Don Quixote cannot see, the companion constantly reminds the reader of those aspects of reality which the refined traveler, for reasons of taste, has chosen to ignore.

The best-known scientific traveler is, of course, Mr. Pickwick, P.C., and the most famous companion, Sam Weller. Because of Dickens' skill, both Pickwick and Sam are drawn with an art which lifts them well above the level of the usual traveler and companion appearing in the humor magazines, but the connection with Dr. Syntax is clearly perceptible, especially in the purpose of the Pickwickian tour and in Mr. Pickwick's ever-ready notebook. Of the artistic travelers, the most familiar is Thackeray's Michael Angelo Titmarsh in the *Paris Sketch Book;* his name itself indicates his place among artists, or at least his aspirations.[9]

The travel-burlesque best exemplifying the conventions current when Twain entered the field is the series of letters entitled "Our Roving Correspondent" which began in the first issue of *Punch* for 1860. Connected to Dr. Syntax by name, profession, and character, the correspondent Jack Easel, art critic, is a man of taste and refinement, at ease in society, at home among the Masters and the monuments of antiquity. Some indication of his pose appears in his comments upon young female tourists in the Italian art galleries (*Punch,* July 27, 1861):

The ease and rapidity with which these charming critics form acquaintance with and discuss the merits of the old Masters is truly astonishing. I once heard a young lady (who certainly did know how to turn her eyes to excellent account) remark, that she had "done" the Capitol between the hours of breakfast and lunch, adding that she would be able to give me a full description of the Borghese Collection by the time we met at dinner. *"Per Bacco!* Ma'am," I exclaimed—you know we were in Italy, and I always ejaculate, if possible, in the language of the country where I am residing—*"per Bacco!* What a muff is your humble servant. Here have I been spending months in the study of a single gallery and am half inclined to throw up my profession in despair, at my ignorance."

His companion is Richard Dewberry, a young man who, according to Mr. Easel's complaint (*Punch,* September 21, 1861), admires the girls more than "the monuments of antiquity." Furthermore, Dick's indifference to the various proprieties causes Easel some mortification:

> "Flirting about the Piazza with pretty girls is all very well," I said, one morning to MR. DEWBERRY, "but as Paterfamilias will naturally expect you to have done something while you are away, I advise you to make notes of what you see, or keep a journal."
> "A journal! Oh, bosh!" politely answers MASTER DICK, (who has a great horror of occupying his time to no profit) "what on earth is the good of a journal? Every muff keeps a journal."

Dick, however, does agree to take lessons in Italian, and Easel is gratified to notice that for several nights Dick has been closeted to a late hour with his tutor. But one morning Easel enters Dick's room after one of these sessions and finds it littered with empty bottles.

Twain undoubtedly was familiar with such travel-burlesques in the English humor magazines, *Punch* and *Fun*.[10] As a practicing humorist he probably read them even before he left Virginia City; English papers, journals, and magazines, including the humor magazines, circulated freely in Nevada.[11] The newsdealers' advertisements in almost every issue of any San Francisco paper attest to the availability and wide circulation of these magazines in the San Francisco area. Twain's acquaintance with the type was, of course, strengthened by his association with Webb, who may have written such burlesques for *Vanity Fair* or at least knew the type from examples published in the magazine. During its brief existence *Vanity Fair* published several travel-burlesques of the Syntax type, the best of which is the series "Our European Letter," which began August 11, 1860. Possibly, too, Twain gained some knowledge of the type from the files of *Hutchings' Illustrated California Magazine* in the *Golden Era* offices. Lawrence and Brooks, owners of the *Golden Era,* purchased the *California Magazine* from Hutchings in 1861, merged it with the *California Mountaineer,* and published it from 1861 to 1864 under the title *California Magazine and Mountaineer* as a monthly collection of *Golden Era* materials and reprints from the files of the two parent magazines. In the first issue of his magazine (1856), Hutchings began a series entitled (with allusions both to Combe and to Poe) "Dr. Dotitdown in Search of the Picturesque, Arabesque, Grotesque and Burlesque." Eager to fill his notebook with truths about man and nature, Dr. Dotitdown, a typical Syntax type of scientific traveler, travels through Europe with a guide reminiscent both of Yusef and Billfinger.

From this background of travel-burlesque, the Mr. Twain–Mr. Brown fiction of the Sandwich Islands letters grew. Mr. Twain is not only a refined gentleman sensible of scenic beauty (presented to his readers as picturesque description) and social propriety; he is also a scientific observer, a collector of "curious" information. In Letter 22 he writes:

We passed behind the cascade and the pyramid, and found the bluff pierced by several cavernous tunnels, whose crooked course we followed about fifty feet, but with no notable result, save that we made a discovery that may be of high interest to men of science. We discovered that the darkness in there was singularly like the darkness observable in other particularly dark places—exactly like it, I thought. I am borne out in this opinion by my comrade, who said he did not believe there was any difference, but if there was, he judged it was in favor of this darkness here.[12]

In the same letter he records a number of legends, in the case of one, that of the chief fourteen or fifteen feet high with the monstrous stone lounge, displaying the gullibility characteristic of Dr. Syntax and his descendants. After carefully noting the dimensions of the stone, "eleven feet four inches long and three feet square at the small end," and its weight, "a few thousand pounds," he finds no reason to doubt the story that the chief carried the stone to its present resting place because "this circumstance is established by the most reliable traditions." The legend also asserts that when the chief reclined on the lounge, "his legs hung down over the end, and when he snored he woke the dead." Again Mr. Twain comments, "These facts are all attested by irrefragible tradition." Although he is not consistently endowed with this characteristic—in his remarks on the next legend, he himself points out the absurdities and thus destroys the illusion—Mr. Twain exhibits a sentimental regard for venerable curiosities which his companion Brown does not share: "I don't say anything against this Injun's inches, but I copper his judgment. He didn't know his own size. Because if he did, why didn't he fetch a rock that was long enough, while he was at it?"

Totally impervious to the beauties of nature, Mr. Brown has no patience with such liberties as those Mr. Twain takes for reasons of taste with the description of Honolulu harbor. A fine example of the picturesque, the landscape is carefully framed by mountains, its foreground tastefully arranged against an artistic background:

I moved in the midst of a summer calm as tranquil as dawn in the Garden of Eden; in the place of our familiar skirting sand hills and the placid bay, I saw on the one side a framework of tall, precipitous mountains close at hand, clad in refreshing green near the shore, bound and bordered by a long white line of foamy spray dashing against the reef, and further out the dead, blue water of the deep sea, flecked with "white caps," and in the far horizon a single, lonely sail—

Brown will have none of this; he interrupts:

"Yes, and hot. Oh, I reckon not (only 82 in the shade)! Go on, now, and put it all down, now that you've begun; just say, 'And more "santipedes," and cockroaches, and fleas, and lizards, and red ants, and scorpions, and spiders, and mosquitoes and missionaries'—oh, blame my cats if I'd live here two months, not if I was High-You-Muck-a-Muck and King of Wawhoo, and had a harem full of hyenas!"

The exchanges typify the relationship between Mr. Twain and Mr. Brown. Despite their companionship the two are extreme opposites in social propriety, sentimentality, language, and perception. The conflict between the two furnishes the structure of the fictive portion of the letters.

Expected to write both humorous fiction and factual reports about the Islands and their resources, Mark Twain faced a peculiar structural problem which he tried to solve in two ways: within individual letters he strove for an alternation of fact and fiction; in the entire series, besides applying the principle of alternation in the grouping of letters, he manipulated the sequence of dispatch so that the series would gradually build up toward and eventually culminate in a climax.

The series consists of twenty-five letters which, when classified according to the predominance of either fact or fiction, fall into distinct groups:

1. Letters 1 and 2: Mr. Twain–Mr. Brown narrative.

2. Letter 3: factual report about the steamer *Ajax*.

3. Letters 4-8: Mr. Twain–Mr. Brown narrative.

4. Letters 9-17: factual reports on whaling, politics, the funeral, and the *Hornet* disaster.

5. Letters 18-22: Mr. Twain–Mr. Brown narrative.

6. Letter 23: factual report on the sugar industry.

7. Letters 24 and 25: Mr. Twain–Mr. Brown narrative, concluding with the visit to the volcano.

The alternation between fiction and factual reporting may at first appear completely accidental; but apparently Twain was conscious of the need for alternation and of the literary effect to be gained from its use. In Letter 6, devoted predominantly to the fiction, he self-consciously writes, "This is a good time to drop in a paragraph of information." The sentence introduces two factual paragraphs after a lengthy episode with the steed Oahu; the two paragraphs are followed by further humor, after which he again writes, "One more yarn, and then I will pass to something else." But the attempt to alternate fact and fiction is most evident in the letters devoted to information about the Islands. Several of these, Letters 3, 10, 11, 12, 14, 15, and 17, are completely factual, the remainder predominantly so, the seriousness relieved, however, by intrusions from "that fellow Brown." For example, Letter 15, devoted to the last night of mourning for the dead princess, is serious in over-all intent, but each section of reportorial description is followed by a short comic intrusion from Brown. These intrusions are different from such interruptions as Brown's while Mr. Twain is describing Honolulu, because they occur not during the writing of the letters but during the action described in the letters.

With the two types of intrusions Twain created a rather complex fiction based on the maintenance of two levels of action. One is the narrative within the letters dealing with the adventures of Mr. Twain and Mr. Brown in the Islands. Some of the factual reports become a part of this fiction through such intrusions as Brown's irreverent remarks during the princess' funeral. The other is the dramatic action occurring during the writing of the narrative, that is, the conflict between the two characters over how the adventures should be presented to the reader. By introducing the second level of action, Twain is able to present the remainder of the factual information, yet at the same moment, through Brown's intrusions, maintain the immediacy of his fiction. Furthermore, he achieves a measure of suspense even in the midst of the most factual report, because for the reader each letter is spiced with the expectation that in the very next paragraph "that fellow Brown" will peep over Mr. Twain's shoulder and address himself directly to the reader. Thus Twain solved a rather difficult problem in construction; he transformed the conventional burlesque relationship between the traveler and his companion into a frame, so to speak, into a "narrative-plank," which permitted the insertion of fact into his fiction without an undue interruption of the narrative. Of course, he did not achieve a perfect work of art in the process, but the solution is ingenious and indicates a rather high level of ability. Even in his first attempt at travel-burlesque, he was learning to manipulate the conventions to his own ends.

In addition to the alternation between fact and fancy, Twain attempted to meet the problem of total effect. He apparently felt his fiction should end in a climax of some sort, for he tried to provide one in his description of Kilauea Volcano. Of the conclusion which Twain devised, G. Ezra Dane writes, "Thus Mark Twain left his Sacramento *Union* readers hanging, like Mahomet's coffin, half-way between earth and sky, on top of Kilauea."[13] Dane is to a certain extent right; the reader is left hanging in mid-air, because, after all, a travel narrative should not end until the voyage does. Twain, however, did not intend to leave such an impression; instead he consciously worked to provide his readers with a conclusion so impressive that a subsequent prosaic return home would be distinctly anticlimactic.

The composition dates reveal an important fact about Twain's intent if the letters are numbered in the order of their appearance in the *Union:*

Letters 1-11: dated March 18, 1866, to April——.
Letters 12 and 13: dated May 23.
Letters 14-22: dated June 22 to July——.
Letter 23: dated September 10.
Letters 24 and 25: dated June—— and June 3rd, Midnight.

The last two letters properly come between Letters 13 and 14, but Twain held them over to the end of his journey. A consideration of the chronology of his trip, the dates of the letters, and the dates of publication in the *Union* reveals the reason.

According to the first letter, Twain sailed from San Francisco March 7, landed in Honolulu on the 18th, and toured Oahu from March 18 until late in April. He then left for a six-weeks' tour of Maui, returning to Honolulu May 22, according to the concluding paragraph of Letter 12, dated May 23: "It has been six weeks since I touched a pen. In explanation and excuse I offer the fact that I spent that time ... on the island of Maui. I only got back yesterday."

In the same paragraph he announces his intended departure for Hawaii the following day, May 24. Furthermore, he promises to write up his notes on the Maui trip at some future time, but he never does. The next letter, also dated May 23, describes a session of the Hawaiian legislature. From May 24 to June 20 or 21 he toured Hawaii and visited Kilauea Volcano. During this time, he wrote Letters 24 and 25, dating them "June——" and "June 3rd, Midnight," but did not dispatch them. On June 22, according to the opening paragraph of Letter 14, he is back in Honolulu: "I have just got back from a three weeks' cruise on the island of Hawaii and an eventful sojourn of several days at the great volcano." Letters 14 to 17 describe the death and burial of the princess and report the *Hornet* disaster. The remainder of the letters, 18 to 25, deal with the Hawaii trip.

What he did after his return to Honolulu about June 21 does not appear in the series. On September 24, fourteen days after he wrote Letter 23 from Honolulu, he is back in San Francisco, for on that date he wrote a letter from San Francisco to the *Daily Hawaiian Herald*.[14] The two letters written during the Hawaiian trip and dated "June—" and "June 3rd, Midnight" were not printed in the *Union* until October 27 and November 17 respectively. Since the usual lapse of time between the date of writing and date of publication for those letters written from Honolulu is from thirty to thirty-four days, Twain apparently kept possession of these two letters and carried them back to San Francisco with him.

Only one reason satisfactorily explains his silence about the events of his Honolulu sojourn after his return from Hawaii and the conscious manipulation revealed by the withholding of the two June letters. Kilauea Volcano evidently made a great impression upon him, causing him, after he had written but before he had dispatched the letters, to conceive the idea of making the visit to the volcano the climax of the series. Therefore, after his return to Honolulu, he wrote four factual letters to meet his obligations as a reporter and then composed a consecutive burlesque series based on the Hawaiian trip and culminating in the spectacular volcano description.

Despite the rearrangement, the reader is, as Dane remarks, left hanging "half-way between earth and sky, on top of Kilauea." A certain formal effect is achieved, but the sense of completion is lost. Twain himself must have recognized the weakness, for when he undertook his next major task, he abandoned the attempt to achieve a climax. He let the actual itinerary furnish the course of his narrative and experimented in other directions. When he left San Francisco for the East, his contract with the *Alta California* called for a series of humorous letters describing his journey by way of the Isthmus to New York. At that time he had no idea that a few months later he would be touring Europe and the Holy Land with the *Quaker City* party. But, although the early letters about the voyage to New York and the *Quaker City* letters are the result of two different contracts, no break appears in the narrative. The whole series may be treated as a single composition.

The initial letter reintroduces the Mr. Twain–Mr. Brown fiction of the Sandwich Islands letters. The first encounter of the two characters on the deck of the *America* shows that neither has changed since they toured Hawaii together. As the steamship backs away from the pier, Mr. Twain's sensibilities are stirred:

> Then I stood apart and soliloquized: "Green be my memories of thee as are thy hills this bright December day, O Mistress of the Occident: May no—"
>
> "Oh, dang the Occident: There's lively times down stairs. The old man played his hand for all it was worth—the passengers raised him —the old man come back—they went him better—the old man passed out, and all things are lovely and the—"
>
> "Say what you have got to say in plain English, Brown, and refrain from vulgar metaphor."

Mr. Brown is still a "bitter enemy to sentiment"; Mr. Twain retains his refinement, his sensitiveness to the picturesque, and—witness the twelfth letter, October 6, 1867—his interest in science.

The series does not differ markedly in technique from the Sandwich Islands letters. The major structural device for the fiction is the Mr. Twain–Mr. Brown relationship, and the two levels of fiction are retained. The sequence of events on the two voyages furnishes direction for the fiction, although Twain apparently did not feel compelled to include every occurrence. The adventures in Marseilles, for example, which fill a large section of *The Innocents Abroad,* are not mentioned in the letters. He still alternates fact and fiction by inserting Brown's intrusions in the midst of factual or descriptive material, but the intrusions comparable to Brown's interruption of Mr. Twain's picturesque description are no longer presented as dramatic action. Instead they come to the reader as paraphrases of or excerpts from Brown's journal or one of his reports. The whole series has a perfunctory air: he is doing what he did in the Sandwich Islands letters with the same competence.

III

Not until he undertook to make the *Quaker City* letters into a book did he resume his experimentation with the travel-burlesque form. Comparison of the *Alta* series with *The Innocents Abroad* shows a number of major changes. Mr. Brown disappears from the list of characters; much new material is added, including a number of condensed burlesques; material is shifted from place to place; but most important of all, a new character replaces the old Mr. Twain, the man of refinement. All these revisions tend in one direction, toward a sharper focus upon the narrator and his consciousness as the unifying element of the book. The one character becomes the medium through which all material reaches the reader. In short, the modifications introduced in *The Innocents Abroad* prepared the way for *Roughing It.*

In his study of Twain's additions in revision of *The Innocents Abroad,* Leon T. Dickinson found that a serious-comic alternation governed the selection and placement of new episodes in the text.[16]

But more interesting is the fact that Twain, in addition to using once again an over-all pattern derived from the burlesque travel narrative, also turned to literary burlesque for new comic material. To the one burlesque in the original series, the Legend of the Seven Sleepers, Twain added two others, the Story of Abelard and Heloise and the Legend of Count Luigi. A third addition, the Roman playbill and the column from the *Roman Daily Battle-Axe,* is not in the strictest sense a literary burlesque because it parodies newspaper drama columns, writing which hardly can be called literature. It is, however, worthy of consideration.

The idea of using such interpolated burlesques apparently first came to Twain during the voyage from Nicaragua to New York, or at least shortly after his arrival in New York. In the notebook draft of his *Alta* letter dated January 12, 1867, he included a parody-burlesque of Victor Hugo's *Les Travailleurs de la mer* entitled "A Novel *Who Was He?*"[16] Written in the condensed form pioneered by Thackeray and used by Webb and Harte, the burlesque is a good parody of Hugo's style and a fair imitation of Hugo's techniques as a novelist. In the finished letter the burlesque was omitted, but its use in the draft letter illustrates by contrast Twain's technical advance when he interpolated the Legend of the Seven Sleepers in Letter 31 from Ephesus and the other burlesques in *The Innocents Abroad.* The Hugo burlesque, in itself fairly good, has no relationship to anything else before or after it in the letter series; the others, appropriate to the region traversed by Twain's narrator, are prompted by some particular building or natural feature encountered on the journey. The Story of Abelard and Heloise grows naturally from the visit to the lovers' tomb in Père Lachaise. The Legend of Count Luigi follows the observation of a medieval ruin visible from the Lecco-Bergamo carriage road. The Coliseum suggests the Roman playbill and the burlesque drama column, and the Cave of the Seven Sleepers in Ephesus calls for a Legend of the Seven Sleepers.

The tone of the first, the Story of Abelard and Heloise,

derives principally from the various puns on the ecclesiastical term
"canon." Heloise's uncle, Fulbert, the canon of the cathedral of
Paris, becomes a "mountain howitzer," an "old gun," a "son of a
gun," an "old swivel," and an "old smooth-bore." Other puns build
upon this military terminology; for example, the canon of the
cathedral is "spiked." The narrator's iconoclasm, the desire to strip
the tale of the "nauseous sentimentality that would enshrine for
our loving worship a dastardly seducer like Pierre Abelard," adds
to the burlesque tone. Apparently the idea of vilifying Abelard
was not original with Twain, but came instead from his source
for the history of Abelard and Heloise, O. W. Wight's *Lives and
Letters of Abelard and Heloise.*[17] The indebtedness to Wight
appears in Twain's attempt to prove Abelard "a cold-hearted villain
... with the deliberate intention of debauching a confiding, innocent
girl." To do so, he quotes what he claims is an excerpt from one
of Abelard's letters:

"I can not cease to be astonished at the simplicity of Fulbert; I was as
much surprised as if he had placed a lamb in the power of a hungry wolf.
Heloise and I, under pretext of study, gave ourselves up wholly to love,
and the solitude that love seeks our studies procured for us. Books were
open before us, but we spoke oftener of love than philosophy, and
kisses came more readily from our lips than words."[18]

Twain's quotation is a greatly edited version of the famous passage
from Abelard's *Historia Calamitatum*:

In qua re quidem quanta ejus simplicitas esset vehementer admiratus,
non minus apud me obstupui, quam si agnam teneram famelico lupo
committeret. Qui quum eam, mihi non solum docendam, verum etiam
vehementer constringendam traderet, quid aliud agebat, quam ut votis
meis licentiam penitus daret, et occasionem, etiam si nollemus, offeret,
ut quam videlicet blanditiis non possem, minis et verberibus facilius
flecterem? Sed duo erant, quae sum maxime a turpi suspicione revoca-
bant, amor videlicet neptis, et continentiae meae fama praeteriat. Quid
plura? primum domo una conjungimur, postmodum animo. Sub
occasione itaque disciplinae amori penibus vacabamus, et secretos

recessus, quos amor optabat, studium lectionis offerebat. Apertis itaque libris plura de amore quam de lectione verba se ingerebant, plura erant oscula quam sententiae.[19]

Twain's version is a fairly fluent rendering of only the first and the two concluding sentences of the original. The intervening material, that which most clearly proves the "deliberate intention of debauching a confiding, innocent girl," is omitted.

Since Twain, untutored in Latin, could not furnish his own translation, presumably he drew upon one of the three sources available at the time he was writing *The Innocents Abroad:* Guizot's *Abailard et Héloise,* Gréard's *Lettres complètes d'Abélard et d'Héloise,* and Wight's English text. Although his French was not fluent, it was, if several practice conjugations, vocabulary lists, and sample sentences in his notebooks are interpreted favorably, sufficient to permit him to puzzle out a few sentences. But his version of the Latin sentence "Sub occasione itaque disciplinae amori penibus vacabamus, et secretos recessus, quos amor optabat, studium lectionis offerebat" cannot have come from either of the two French versions. Guizot translates the passage, "Sous le prétexte de l'étude, nous étions tout entiers à l'amour. Loin de tous les regards, l'amour s'applaudissait de nos retraites studieuses."[20] Gréard writes, "Sous prétexte d'étudier, nous étions donc tout entiers à l'amour; ces mysterieux entretiens, que l'amour appelait de ses voeux, les leçons nous en ménageaient l'occasion."[21] Twain's version, however, reads, "Heloise and I, under pretext of study, gave ourselves up wholly to love, and the solitude that love seeks our studies procured for us," a version very close to Wight's: "Under the pretext of study, we were wholly free for love, and the retirement which love sought, zeal for reading offered."[22]

The burlesque does strip the legend of its "nauseous sentimentality," but Twain's version is not much better because he has replaced the sentiment with a punctilious rectitude inimical to burlesque, which is neither moral nor immoral but amoral. Undoubtedly some of what Paine would call the "righteous wrath against wrong" comes from Twain's own tendency to see life in solid blacks and whites, but a portion comes from his source. Introducing the passage from the *Historia Calamitatum*, Wight comments, "We cannot help cursing Abelard, notwithstanding all the extenuating circumstances of his times, for his sin was a deliberate act, as appears from his own confession." Twain goes much further in condemnation, ignoring the extenuating circumstances and calling Abelard "a cold-hearted villain." A similar exaggeration appears in the characterization of Fulbert. Wight says, "Fulbert loves money, and is tempted with the price offered. He loves his niece, too, and thinks it is a good opportunity to complete her education under the private instruction of the most renowned teacher."[23] Twain puts the two ideas, love of money and love of niece, together into a distortion of Wight's version: "The good old swivel saw here a rare opportunity; his niece, whom he so much loved, would absorb knowledge from this man, and it would not cost him a cent. Such was Fulbert—penurious." Only in the case of Heloise does Wight outdo Twain. Of her Twain writes, "I have not a word to say against the misused, faithful girl, and would not withhold from her grave a single one of those simple tributes which blighted youths and maidens offer to her memory." But Wight becomes maudlin:

We weep for thee, fallen Heloise! Thy spirit has found the sympathy for which it longed, but delirium flows swiftly in thy blood, and paints upon thy youthful cheek the crimson of sin.... We pity thee, but cannot greatly blame; the earth is cursed beneath thee, but heaven, with its mercy, is above thee still![24]

The moralistic quality in Twain's burlesque robs it of much of its effectiveness today.

The second interpolated burlesque, the Legend of Count Luigi, is much better. Inserted in Chapter XXI of *The Innocents Abroad*, it is evoked by the sight of "many a gray old medieval castle, clad thick with ivy that swung its green banners down from towers and turrets where once some old Crusader's flag had floated."[25] Twain quite possibly intended to connect it with a particular landmark on the Lecco-Venice carriage road. The name of the chief character, Count Luigi Gennaro Guido Alphonso de Genova, may conceal a reference to Count Luigi Avogardo de Genova, who defended Brescia against the Chevalier de Bayard. The actual Count Luigi's castle stands on a height outside Brescia a short distance east of Bergamo on the road to Venice. If such a reference was indeed intended, Twain misplaces the castle, for the narrator comes upon it west of Bergamo.

The first half of the legend seems most indebted to Thackeray's *Legend of the Rhine,* a burlesque of Dumas's *Otto, l'archer.* Like Count Ludwig in Thackeray's burlesque, Count Luigi goes off to the crusades and returns after a long lapse of time to learn from a peasant that all is not well at the castle. Count Ludwig's helmet and shield device is the sword Excalibur; Count Luigi earned renown on the battlefield with "his good Excalibur." And like Thackeray, Twain uses to good effect the humorous device of scrambled medieval terms: "...one mild September morning, armed with battle-axe, portcullis and thundering culverin, he rode through the greaves and bucklers of his donjonkeep with as gallant a troop of Christian bandits as ever stepped in Italy."[26]

The second portion of the legend, the treachery of the "cruel Leonardo," is an original burlesque of two plays by Victor Hugo, *Lucrezia Borgia* and *Angelo.* The "versatile and talented Ugolino" thinly disguises a reference to Hugo, himself. The "justly celebrated Rodolpho" and the "gifted and accomplished Roderigo" are characters from *Angelo;* Gennero, Lucrezia, and Alphonso are characters from *Lucrezia Borgia.* In the burlesque, the entry of the "robed and close-cowled" harlequins into Leonardo's presence is based upon the solemn procession of chanting monks filing in and lining the walls of the doomed Gennero's chamber in *Lucrezia Borgia.* In fact, the leader of the "harlequins" is called "the chief monk."

In addition to the more or less general burlesque, Twain manages to poke fun at two particular scenes from *Angelo*. Lucrezia's emphatic "NE-VER!" in the legend reflects Rodolfo's equally emphatic "Jamais!" in the play. The final scene of the legend burlesques the recognition scene and tableau in *Angelo:*

> La Tisbe, à part: Ciel! O ma mère!
> (La porte du fond s'ouvre. Angelo paraît vêtu d'une robe de nuit.)
> Catarine, revenant sur le devant du théâtre: Mon mari! Je suis perdu!

In the legend this dialogue becomes:

> "Oh, God, Oh, God, my husband!"
> "Oh, God, Oh, God, my wife!"
> "My father!"
> "My precious!" [Tableau.]

No evidence clearly indicates when or how Twain became acquainted with *Angelo,* but he could have seen *Lucrezia Borgia* before he sailed on the *Quaker City* because the play was quite popular in New York in 1867. Probably, however, his acquaintance was with a theatrical burlesque of *Lucrezia,* not with the play itself. During the 1866-67 season, the various local burlesque troupes and the touring San Francisco Minstrels produced four popular burlesques of *Lucrezia Borgia*.[27] Twain probably saw the Minstrels' version, for he was a frequent visitor at their theater, according to his *Alta California* letter for June 16, 1867: "Every night of their lives, they play to packed houses—every single seat full and dozens of people standing up. I have good reason to know, because I have been there pretty often." Certainly the theater was in his mind when he put into Luigi's mouth the typical language of nineteenth-century theater managers: "Good my lord, in acrobatic feats, in practice with the dumb-bells, in balancing and ground and lofty tumbling are we versed—and sith your highness asketh me, I venture here to publish that in the truly marvelous and entertaining Zampillaerostation—"[28]

Twain's interest in and knowledge of the theater are reflected once again in the Roman playbill and the drama column from the *Roman Daily Battle-Axe.* The playbill, of course, parodies the grandiloquent language of theater announcements, and the drama column parodies just such columns as Twain himself had written in San Francisco. Although the burlesque review is not a literary burlesque, it does furnish additional evidence of Twain's skill as a parodist.

Similarly, the Legend of the Seven Sleepers further illustrates Mark Twain's skill in parody, for this time he parodies biblical language and produces such pseudo-biblical eloquence as "And they said, Depart thou to Hades, and went their way." The biblical associations surrounding Ephesus and its environs may have suggested the use of such a style, but evidence within the burlesque suggests that Twain is actually parodying the language of Sunday-school literature. At the very beginning of the legend, he confesses, "I am telling this story for nice little boys and girls," a fairly obvious reference to the same sort of literature he burlesques in "The Story of the Bad Little Boy." In the mixture of styles is further evidence, for mingled with the pseudo-biblical language are such typical fairy-story phrases as "once upon a time," "the good King Maximilianus," "by-and-by," and "they traveled in many lands, and had many strange adventures." But perhaps the best evidence is in the direction taken by the burlesque. The seven sleepers, originally marvels of Christian piety and purity, become the exact opposite. In the original legend, the seven young men decided to leave Ephesus rather than stay and be forced to worship heathen gods; they sold all their goods and distributed the profits among the poor. Twain's seven prove prodigies in the light-fingered art when they leave town.

All these burlesques are important for several reasons already mentioned: they illustrate Twain's skill as a parodist; they further illustrate his desire to achieve a serious-comic contrast, and because each is appropriate to the serious description preceding it, they reveal a measure of integration in the fiction. The Roman playbill and drama column is of additional importance, because it reveals a further step in structural integration. The three legends, Abelard and Heloise, Count Luigi, and the Seven Sleepers, are, in a sense, superimposed upon the narrative. That is, the narrator merely transmits them to the reader as narratives within the narrative. Attributing them to "history" or a garrulous Italian coachman, he assumes no personal responsibility for them. Physically, each is separated from the rest of the text by a caption. But the discovery of the Roman playbill and drama column is presented as a personal experience:

For me was reserved the high honor of discovering among the rubbish of the ruined Coliseum the only playbill of that establishment now extant. There was a suggestive smell of mint-drops about it still, a corner of it had evidently been chewed, and on the margin, in choice Latin, these words were written in a delicate female hand....

In this case, the events within the burlesque are still beyond the personal experience of the narrator, and typographically the burlesque is separated from the rest of the text. But the narrator himself becomes the authority for the burlesque; so far as the reader is concerned the burlesque exists only in the consciousness of the narrator.

The major change made in revising the *Alta* letters to form *The Innocents Abroad* involved the characters Mr. Twain and Mr. Brown. In his study of *The Innocents Abroad,* Mr. Dickinson concentrates upon the disappearance of Brown, attributing it to Twain's desire to remove the vulgarity from his text. He writes, "What happened ... is that many of Brown's remarks, usually the vulgar ones, Clemens dropped. But he retained the comments that reflect Brown's ignorance; in the book, however, they are attributed not to Brown but to a 'thoughtful old Pilgrim,' to Jack, and, most often, to Blucher." But the removal of vulgarity does not necessitate the total excision of the character. One is entitled to ask why Twain did not merely eliminate the vulgarity. Mr. Dickinson attempts an answer in a footnote:

At times...the character of Brown is merged with that of Clemens' assumed character, Mark Twain. Clemens had used Brown originally as a mouthpiece for his cruder and more inane remarks. But as time went on, he gave up most of the crude ones; and as he developed the character of Mark Twain, he himself...could utter the inanities. It is for this reason chiefly that Brown disappears from Clemens' writing.[29]

Mr. Dickinson fails, however, to make an essential distinction between the name and the characteristics of the character. Although the name *Brown* disappears from the final text, most of his characteristics do not; what is more important, the name *Twain* remains, but the original characteristics of Mr. Twain are so well deleted that only a few traces of his refinement, sentiment, and taste are left. A study of the Mr. Twain–Mr. Brown deletions shows they were made, not primarily to remove vulgarity, but to eliminate the Mr. Twain–Mr. Brown contrast, the distinction between the refined character and his troublesome companion.[30] For example, the scientific experiment with the dog reported in the *Alta* letter for October 6, 1867, disappears because the humor depends upon Mr. Twain's desire to make a contribution to science, a desire frustrated by his companion's insensibility to such noble aims: "[Brown] swore at me, too, for wanting to take so much trouble just to try some foolish experiment. This person has no appreciation of science." Similarly Brown's comment about the Pope in the *Alta* letter for November 6, 1867, is dropped because it has no point without Mr. Twain's answering comment, "These things distress me beyond expression."

The elimination of Mr. Twain greatly strengthens the book. In the original letters, unable to keep his hands off Brown's role, Twain occasionally forgot or ignored the character distinctions required by his fiction and starred the narrator in a role properly belonging to Brown. For example, as Brown's mentor in refined language, Mr. Twain frequently must correct his companion's grammar and diction; but when Mr. Twain goes to the offices of the *Quaker City* tour, not with Brown but with an unnamed *Tribune* reporter, the reporter assumes the function usually allotted to Mr. Twain, and Mr. Twain exhibits the characteristic Brownisms in his speech.[31] During the conversation with the tour official, the *Tribune* man has to warn Mr. Twain, "Oh, devil take it, don't use those villainous slang expressions—you'll expose everything." A second time he whispers, "Oh, d—n it! ... you'll ruin everything with that slang." Furthermore, to maintain a fiction of dramatic conflict between two narrators on the matter of narration is difficult. Ingenious, but never very successful, the conception of Brown as an alternate narrator poses difficult problems in point of view. Twain tried to solve the problem first by permitting Mr. Twain to quote Brown's expostulations directly, later by having him reproduce sections from Brown's reports and journals. But Mr. Twain is always the narrator most immediate to the reader's consciousness. In all respects, Twain's solution, the creation of a new narrator whose mind is the only medium through which the narrative reaches the reader, is best.

The new narrator is neither the Mr. Twain nor the Mr. Brown of the earlier narratives; although he retains more of Mr. Brown's characteristics, he is actually a combination of the two. As a result he becomes in himself an important structural device. Like the earlier refined traveler, he is the agency through which Twain interpolates burlesques into the narrative, but he has become something more in at least two episodes. The refined traveler accepts unquestioningly the legends, tales, and histories he happens to hear. The duty of doubting devolves upon his companion. The narrator in *The Innocents Abroad* accepts the Roman playbill and the Legend of the Seven Sleepers without demur. But after investigating the "true" history of Abelard and Heloise, he bemoans the sentiment he has, in his ignorance, wasted upon the memory of Abelard and vows to investigate such sentimental legends more thoroughly before he gives them any "tearful attentions." At the end of the Legend of Count Luigi, he comments, "Splendid legend—splendid lie—drive on." When he learns that Bergamo is the birthplace of harlequin, the legend acquires new meaning for him, presumably because now he knows what attitude to take toward it. In these two episodes the narrator undergoes a process of education or, in the case of Abelard, of disillusionment: he himself becomes the doubter after learning the "truth." In other words, he becomes the authority not only for the fiction but for the fact which follows and explicates the fiction.

In eliminating the Mr. Twain–Mr. Brown contrast, Twain made two sacrifices: he gave up the character conflict of the Sandwich Islands and *Alta* letters and the intrinsic if poorly preserved consistency of his earlier narrator. Of the two, the greater was the surrender of the conflict, for he deprived himself of his "narrative-plank." No longer a refined traveler, the narrator of *The Innocents Abroad* shares the unregeneracy of the old Mr. Brown with his companions, Dan, Jack, Blucher, and the doctor. One of a group known as the Sinners, he does not as an individual figure consistently in any conflict with another character. Twain partially mitigates the loss of his character-axis by substituting for it an embryonic antagonism between the Sinners and the other passengers, the Pilgrims. That such an antagonism did in fact exist is clear from Twain's *Herald* letter of November 20, 1867, and from the recriminations it provoked.[32] But Twain exaggerates the cleavage between the two groups. The ebullience of Twain and his friends becomes irreverence. Like Mr. Brown, the Sinners are impious, intemperate, unsentimental, and above all ignorant of the deportment proper for travelers making the Grand Tour and a pilgrimage to the Holy Land. None of the individual Sinners consistently displays these characteristics, but the group does in its relationships with the other passengers. Similarly the restraint of the Pilgrims becomes a gravity befitting the old Mr. Twain. Both the exaggerated solemnity of the Pilgrims and the embryonic antagonism of the fiction appear in the description of the "Pilgrim" bird in the Marseilles zoo:

> In the great Zoölogical Gardens, we found...a sort of tall, long-legged bird with a beak like a powder-horn, and close-fitting wings like the tails of a dress coat. This fellow stood up with his eyes shut and his shoulders stooped forward a little, and looked as if he had his hands under his coat tails. Such tranquil stupidity, such supernatural gravity, such self-righteousness, and such ineffable self-complacency as were in the countenance and attitude of that gray-bodied, dark-winged, bald-headed, and preposterously uncomely bird! He was so ungainly, so pimply about the head, so scaly about the legs; yet so serene, so unspeakably satisfied! He was the most comical-looking creature that can be imagined. It was good to hear Dan and the doctor laugh—such natural and such enjoyable laughter had not been heard among our excursionists since our ship sailed away from America. This bird was a god-send to us, and I should be an ingrate if I forgot to make honorable mention of him in these pages. Ours was a pleasure excursion; therefore we stayed with that bird an hour, and made the most of him. We stirred him up occasionally, but he only unclosed an eye and slowly closed it again, abating no jot of his stately piety of demeanor or his tremendous seriousness. He only seemed to say, "Defile not Heaven's anointed with unsanctified hands." We did not know his name, and so we called him "The Pilgrim."[33]

The Sinner-Pilgrim conflict is a promising substitute for the earlier character-axis, but Twain did not take advantage of its potentialities, possibly because of the protests aroused by his *Herald* letter. Appearing only sporadically, it is not presented as dramatic action. Consequently, it contributes little to the structure of the book.

Because the major portion of the book describes the travels of the Sinners, not their conflict with the Pilgrims, the new narrator left Twain with no clear-cut distinctions among the characters involved in the dramatic action such as those differentiating Mr. Twain and Mr. Brown. To supply the lack, he occasionally fell back upon the old Twain-Brown contrast for structure within episodes. For example, when Dan, the doctor, and the narrator land at Marseilles, Dan, ignorant in French and inexperienced as a traveler, plays the role of the old Mr. Brown; the narrator and the doctor, "fluent" in the language and "wise" in the ways of foreigners, together perform the function of Mr. Twain.

One result of the revision, then, is the introduction of some marked inconsistencies in the character of the narrator, despite the greater unity provided by the single point of view. Actually, the new narrator performs three different functions, appearing at times as Mr. Twain in episodes with other Sinners, as Mr. Brown in the Sinner-Pilgrim conflict, and as reporter in the presentation of factual material to the reader. The three functions result in the expression of three conflicting attitudes toward each of various specific subjects. The travel-worn joke about journals appears early in the book, in Chapter IV, when the narrator, like the old Mr. Twain, urges young Jack to keep at his journal. Almost immediately, the attitude of the reporter appears in the comment, "If you wish to inflict a heartless and malignant punishment upon a young person, pledge him to keep a journal a year." On the return home, the Sinner, the descendant of Mr. Brown, quotes a passage from his boyhood journal and comments, "I stopped, then, discouraged.... That journal finished me. I never have had the nerve to keep one since. My loss of confidence in myself in that line was permanent." The Sinner claims never to have kept a journal since his boyhood, but Clemens, reporter, has just quoted at length from his journal of the *Quaker City* tour![34]

A similar contradiction appears in various comments about picturesque description. Using the technique employed in the Sandwich Islands letters, a picturesque description followed by a devastating comment by Brown or an eloquent action by the steed Oahu, Twain presents the description of Marseilles harbor in the language of the refined traveler:

Toward nightfall, the next evening, we steamed into the great artificial harbor of this noble city of Marseilles, and saw the dying sunlight gild its clustering spires and ramparts, and flood its leagues of environing verdure with a mellow radiance that touched with an added charm the white villas that flecked the landscape far and near.

But deprived of the services of Mr. Brown, Twain must supply his own deflation; in brackets at the end he writes, "Copyright secured according to law." The Sinner's attitude on picturesque description is most evident in his reaction to the Pilgrims' eloquence about the "picturesque" Nazarene girls:

A pilgrim—the "Enthusiast"—said: "See that tall, graceful girl! look at the Madonna-like beauty of her countenance!"
Another pilgrim came along presently and said: "Observe that tall, graceful girl; what queenly Madonna-like gracefullness of beauty is in her countenance."
I said: "She is not tall, she is short; she is not beautiful, she is homely; she is graceful enough, I grant, but she is rather boisterous."

Annoyed by the liberties taken with observed reality, the reporter is unsympathetic with picturesque descriptions found in other books about Palestine. He quotes two descriptions of the area around Galilee and comments:

I have given two fair, average specimens of the character of the testimony offered by the majority of the writers who visit this region. One says, "Of the beauty of the scene I can not say enough," and then proceeds to cover up with a woof of glittering sentences a thing which, when stripped for inspection, proves to be only an unobtrusive basin of water, some mountainous desolation, and one tree. The other, after a conscientious effort to build a terrestrial paradise out of the same materials, with the addition of a "grave and stately stork," spoils it all by blundering upon the ghastly truth at the last.[35]

The characteristic attitude of the refined Syntax-type traveler appears several times when the narrator poses as a man of science, most notably in the visit to the Church of the Holy Sepulchre where he sees a column marking the exact center of the earth. After quoting the evidence sustaining the authenticity of the column, he adds his own contribution to science by bolstering the evidence with some of his own: "the fact that from under this very column was taken the *dust from which Adam was made.*" After pointing out the import of this fact, he concludes: "This will strike any reflecting mind forcibly. That Adam was formed of dirt procured in this very spot is amply proven by the fact that in six thousand years no man has ever been able to prove that the dirt was *not* procured here whereof he was made." The attitudes derived from Mr. Brown make him harder to convince when he visits the Chapel of St. John the Baptist where he sees a marble chest containing the ashes of St. John and, around the chest, the chain with which the saint was bound. Although he desires to believe, the skeptic in him will not be quiet:

We did not desire to disbelieve these statements, and yet we could not feel certain that they were correct—partly because we could have broken that chain, and so could St. John, and partly because we had seen St. John's ashes before, in another church. We could not bring ourselves to think St. John had two sets of ashes.

Similarly the reporter's attitudes rob the narrator of conviction when he relates the visit to the Roman catacombs. For purposes of comment, he quotes several passages from "a book published in New York in 1858, and written by 'Rev. William H. Neligan, LL.D., M.A., Trinity College, Dublin; Member of the Archaeological Society of Great Britain.' "[36] Of Neligan's account of the miracle associated with the remains of St. Joseph Calasanctius, he writes:

To read that in a book written by a monk far back in the Middle Ages, would surprise no one; it would sound natural and proper; but when it is seriously stated in the middle of the nineteenth century, by a man of finished education, an LL.D., M.A., and an Archaeological magnate, it sounds strangely enough. Still, I would gladly change my unbelief for Neligan's faith, and let him make the conditions as hard as he pleased.

His concluding comment is a direct refutation of the pose usually assumed by the Syntax-type traveler when dealing with such phenomena: "The old gentleman's undoubting, unquestioning simplicity has a rare freshness about it in these matter-of-fact railroading and telegraphing days."

The matter of sentimental tears comes up at three different stages of the journey, each instance revealing a different attitude. The man who visits the tomb of Adam is the same who broke into apostrophe in the valley of bones in the Sandwich Islands. This time the tears flow freely:

The fountain of my filial affection was stirred to its profoundest depths, and I gave way to tumultuous emotion. I leaned upon a pillar and burst into tears. I deem it no shame to have wept over the grave of my poor dead relative. Let him who would sneer at my emotion close this volume here, for he will find little to his taste in my journeyings through Holy Land.

The last sentence reminds the reader of the earlier quotation from William C. Prime's book:

Then once more I bowed my head. It is no shame to have wept in Palestine. I wept when I saw Jerusalem, I wept when I lay in the starlight at Bethlehem, I wept on the blessed shores of Galilee.... Let him who would sneer at my emotion close this volume here, for he will find little to his taste in my journeyings through Holy Land.[37]

The attitudes of the reporter, however, govern the narrator when he views these places; in fact, he finds tears inappropriate in the extreme:

I record it here as a notable but not discreditable fact that not even our pilgrims wept.... There was no call for tears. Tears would have been out of place. The thoughts Jerusalem suggests are full of poetry, sublimity, and more than all, dignity. Such thoughts do not find their appropriate expression in the emotions of the nursery.

Not averse to tears but quite vexed when he discovers his tears have been wasted upon an unworthy subject, a subject such as

Abelard, the narrator exhibits the attitudes of Brown at Père Lachaise. Of Abelard's and Heloise's tomb, he says, "Go when you will, you find somebody snuffling over that tomb." He too had visited the tomb, snuffled, left his immortelles and, in lieu of a bouquet, a bunch of radishes. When he discovers the true story of Abelard and Heloise, he finds he has wasted "a good deal of marketable sentiment very unnecessarily." Unlike Mr. Twain, the sentimentalist, he will ration his tears; unlike Clemens, the reporter, he will not scorn tears:

> The tons of sentiment I have wasted on that unprincipled humbug, in my ignorance! I shall throttle down my emotions hereafter, about this sort of people, until I have read them up and know whether they are entitled to any tearful attentions or not. I wish I had my immortelles back, now, and that bunch of radishes.

Such conflicting attitudes reveal the structural problem resulting from the merger of three different characters, Mr. Twain, Mr. Brown, and the reporter, into one narrator. In the conventional Syntax-derived travel-burlesque, no character corresponding to the reporter is necessary. The refined traveler relates all which good taste permits; the unregenerate companion makes certain that what the traveler ignores is also reported. In effect, each character gives half of the observed reality, the two together accounting for the whole. After merging Mr. Twain and Mr. Brown, Twain had no means of reporting the total reality easily and clearly without introducing a third element into the narrator: the reporter. The difficulty appears most clearly in the discussion of picturesque descriptions of the Holy Land. In the conventional burlesque, the refined traveler would see and report what William C. Prime saw, the writer using sufficient exaggeration in style or details to form a parody or burlesque of Prime's descripton. The companion would then point out all the unpicturesque elements of the scene which the refined traveler had chosen to ignore. Twain, deprived of such a character relationship, must replace the refined traveler's report with quotations from Prime's book. Then, so that his readers may be able to judge Prime's incompetence, he must slip into the role of reporter and describe the scene as accurately as possible, pointing out the disparity between the picturesque description and the actuality.

The problem posed by the merger of Mr. Twain and Mr. Brown, how to retain the exaggerated refinement of the one and the exaggerated rudeness of the other in a single narrator, is difficult. Hints of an answer appear in the Abelard-Heloise and Count Luigi episodes. If the narrator is one who has developed from one attitude to the other as a result of the experiences narrated, the inconsistencies characteristic of the narrator of *The Innocents Abroad* become virtues, for the contrasts in attitudes can be used to mark the various stages of growth. The expansion of such a developmental theme to cover an entire book forms the structural basis of *Roughing It,* the almost complete realization of a new type of narrative which can no longer be termed travel-burlesque. By introducing the principle of growth to account for his narrator's altered attitudes, Twain transformed the narrator himself into a narrative-plank.

IV

In his study of *Roughing It,* Henry Nash Smith has demonstrated that "the pronoun 'I' links two quite different personae: the tenderfoot setting out across the Plains, and the old-timer, the veteran, who has seen the elephant and now looks back upon his own callow days of inexperience." The resulting contrast between callowness and maturity is, in effect, an implicit judgment upon the tenderfoot's ignorance.[38] An important result of the linkage in the prououn "I" of the two different points of view is to eliminate any conflict between the instructive and humorous portions of the book. The reader, viewing the tenderfoot through the eyes of the old-timer, accepts the instructive portions as information furnished by the old-timer to aid the reader in perceiving the callowness and ignorance of the tenderfoot. With such a simple but extremely important device, Twain brings to most of *Roughing It* a unity lacking in the previous narratives. Unity is lost, however, the moment the narrator boards the *Ajax* to sail to Honolulu. As Mr. Smith points out, the last half of the second volume, that portion dealing with the trip to Hawaii, was added at the last moment to fill out the two volumes necessary for a subscription publication. Apparently Twain hastily gathered and edited the Sandwich Islands letters and spliced them upon his narrative in order to meet the terms of his contract, attempting to bring the series into line with the rest of the book by removing Mr. Twain entirely, distributing some of Brown's comments and adventures among several characters, including the new narrator, and eliminating other evidences of Brown entirely. The result, something quite similar in point of view to *The Innocents Abroad,* appears best in the new version of the picturesque view of Honolulu harbor; Twain repeats the description contained in the original letter, but, lacking Mr. Brown, he must devise a new interruption:

...a single, lonely sail—a mere accent-mark to emphasize a slumberous calm and a solitude that were without sound or limit. When the sun sunk down—the one intruder from other realms and persistent in suggestions of them—it was tranced luxury to sit in the perfumed air and forget that there was any world but these enchanted islands.

It was such ecstasy to dream and dream—till you got a bite. A scorpion bite. Then the first duty was to get up out of the grass. . . .

In the new version, that is, Twain uses the seated narrator's vulnerability to the scorpion's bite to introduce the discomforts of which Brown had complained. Taken by itself, the revision is excellent, but in the course of changing the original series to meet the demands of the new character Twain had to sacrifice the dual point of view which unifies *Roughing It* up to the beginning of the Sandwich Islands material. Because the point of view has now become solely that of the unsuspecting tourist, the reader is deprived of any foreshadowing by an old-timer. The single point of view governs the remainder of the book and makes it technically inferior to the preceding sections. For this reason the discussion of the craftsmanship displayed in *Roughing It* will be confined to Volume I and Chapters I through XX of Volume II.

As Mr. Smith points out, "The opening chapters emphasize the callowness and ignorance of the two tenderfeet (the narrator and his brother) who are setting out upon their adventures."[39] But at the same time, they also emphasize the maturity and wisdom of the old-timer. In the first paragraph the narrator looks back upon himself at the outset of the journey and comments, "I was young and ignorant, and I envied my brother." The reader is intended to catch the implication that now, at the moment of writing the book, the narrator is older and wiser. The implication becomes explicit before the first paragraph ends, for the reader learns that "ten or twelve years" have elapsed since the young traveler set forth and that the old-timer's experience in the West is the result not of a brief glimpse but rather of long residence there:

I only proposed to stay in Nevada three months—I had no thought of staying longer than that. I meant to see all I could that was new and strange, and then hurry home to business. I little thought that I would not see the end of that three-month pleasure excursion for six or seven uncommonly long years!

With the reassurance that his guide is a man with "six or seven uncommonly long years" of experience, the reader is ready to watch the "young and ignorant" private secretary to the Secretary of Nevada Territory go through his initiation in the West and develop into the old-timer.

Not merely a callow and ignorant youth, the tenderfoot is a traveler filled with notions of romance and sentiment. Like the Mr. Twain of the Sandwich Islands letters, he is a man of culture and refinement capable of appreciating

scholarly savages ... fittingly associated with backwoodsmen who divide
each sentence into two equal parts; one part critically grammatical,
refined, and choice of language, and the other part just such an attempt to
talk like a hunter or a mountaineer as a Broadway clerk might make
after eating an edition of Emerson Bennett's works and studying frontier
life at the Bowery Theater a couple of weeks.[40]

A man of feeling, he is moved by the sight of the Mormon women,
and his eyes fill with "generous moisture." But more important
is the fact that his ignorance is the ignorance not of artlessness
but of misconception: he is deluded as a result of his reading.
As he comments upon meeting the Goshoots, he is "a disciple
of Cooper and a worshiper of the Red Men—even of the scholarly
savages in the *Last of the Mohicans*." A reader of Emerson
Bennett's works, he confesses he has viewed the Indian "through
the mellow moonshine of romance." As a consequence of such
literature, he has formed a number of preconceived notions about
the West and even about details of survival when "roughing it."
When he, Ollendorff, and Ballou are lost in the snowstorm and
attempt to light a fire with a pistol, he remarks,

Not a man in the party doubted that it *could* be done, and without any
trouble—because every man in the party had read about it in books
many a time and had naturally come to believe it, with trusting simplicity, just as he had long ago accepted and believed *that other* common
book-fraud about Indians and lost hunters making a fire by rubbing
two dry sticks together.

The old-timer's scorn for such book-inspired notions, betrayed
in such phrases as "trusting simplicity" and "common book-
fraud," characterizes him as just such a "bitter enemy to sentiment" as Brown had been. In a sense then, the tenderfoot and
the old-timer reproduce the Mr. Twain–Mr. Brown character-
axis, but because of the introduction of the time element, the
interposition of the journey which accounts for the shift from
tenderfoot to old-timer, the contrasting attitudes do not conflict

as in *The Innocents Abroad*. The old-timer controls both the point of view of the reader and the sentimental character, implicitly ridiculing him and all that has formed him. In the chronicle of the tenderfoot's growth into the old-timer, the book recapitulates that shift in the narrator's character from refined traveler to Sinner which we have been tracing.

As a result of the tenderfoot's bookish expectations and the old-timer's scorn, *Roughing It* becomes not merely "the education of an innocent,"[41] but also a burlesque of the books the innocent has read. Both in general outline and specific details in that portion of *Roughing It* which he could plan carefully, Twain used the alternation of burlesque and fact to control his narrative. In the first chapter, the general plan of the book is summarized in the tenderfoot's prevision of his brother's trip West. The prevision is both an outline of *Roughing It* and a highly condensed burlesque of other narratives of Western adventure:

Pretty soon he would be hundreds and hundreds of miles away on the great plains and deserts, and among the mountains of the Far West, and would see buffaloes and Indians, and prairie-dogs, and antelopes, and have all kinds of adventures, and maybe get hanged or scalped, and have ever such a fine time, and write home and tell us all about it, and be a hero. And he would see the gold-mines and the silver-mines, and maybe go about of an afternoon when his work was done, and pick up two or three pailfuls of shining slugs and nuggets of gold and silver on the hillside. And by and by he would become very rich, and return home by sea, and be able to talk as calmly about San Francisco and the ocean and "the isthmus" as if it was nothing of any consequence to have seen those marvels face to face.

The prevision departs from the actual outline of *Roughing It* only in the detail about the return home. The departure probably indicates Twain's original plans for the conclusion of the book.[42]

The difference between the tenderfoot's forecast and the actuality of his journey is in the disappointment of each expectation. The young traveler participates in a buffalo hunt, but the noble chase turns into "disaster and disgrace" when the wounded bull trees Bemis. He sees prairie dogs and antelopes but in the same passage (Chapter V) he encounters the coyote, the description of which, as Mr. Smith points out, restates the initiation theme of the book. He expects Noble Red Men and finds Goshoots instead. He looks for romantic desperadoes and encounters Slade, who shoots men in cold blood and dies whimpering on the gallows. Indeed, he watches with fascination while "Arkansas" prepares to murder Johnson only to see Arkansas collapse under a woman's tongue-lashing. He finds millions of dollars worth of gold glittering and winking in a stream bed and learns about fool's gold. At last, he reaches San Francisco, but instead of walking the streets a rich man, he becomes a "very adept at 'slinking.' "

The nature of the literature which has molded the young traveler's concept of the Far West can best be ascertained by a study of the burlesque episodes Twain has worked into the narrative. In a sense all the adventures of the tenderfoot are burlesques because they serve to deflate his grandiose dreams. For example, the encounter with the Mexican Plug occasions a violent readjustment of the tenderfoot's ideas about horsemanship. His description of the Californian and Mexican horsemen abounds with the language of romance: "wild, free, magnificent horsemanship," "these picturesquely-clad Mexicans, Californians, and Mexicanized Americans," "easy and nonchalant," "swept through the town like the wind," and "gallantly and gracefully." He pictures himself riding in a similar fashion and resolves to buy a horse. Like many a romance hero before him, he vaults into the saddle only to have all romantic notions about horsemanship jolted out of his system by the Genuine Mexican Plug. Such episodes may be called burlesques only because the entire book may be called a burlesque of Far Western romances, but three episodes within the books—Bemis and the buffalo, the return from the Humboldt, and the *Weekly Occidental* venture—are so fully developed as to constitute burlesques in a stricter sense. Analogous to the burlesques in *The Innocents Abroad,* they are unified episodes within the main narrative, but they achieve a greater measure of integration because not only are they appropriate to the setting and theme as in *The Innocents Abroad,* they also masquerade as actual experiences of the tenderfoot and his companions. Of the three episodes, the least well integrated is the story of the *Weekly Occidental* because, although it purports to be the account of a literary paper in Virginia City upon which the narrator works, it is nevertheless essentially a condensed burlesque of a type of literature totally unconnected with the Far West. The other two, however, burlesque specific themes of Far Western romances.

The story of Bemis' encounter with the buffalo bull is both a tall tale and a burlesque of the sort of literature which led the tenderfoot in his prevision of the West to anticipate with relish the sight of "buffaloes and Indians, and prairie-dogs, and antelopes." Several things within the episode point to the literature upon which it is a burlesque commentary. First is the fact that, when Bemis is thrown from the horse, he "fell at the foot of the only solitary tree there was in nine counties adjacent." Another is the almost diabolical intelligence of the buffalo bull, an intelligence that ranges from the solution of tree-climbing problems to mind-reading. Finally and probably most revealing of all is the miraculous resourcefulness of Bemis not only in stratagem, but also in equipment.

Behind these three salient features of the Bemis story lies an interesting chapter in the history of the western prairies. During most of the nineteenth century, the American West was to the big-game hunter what the African veld is today. One of the first of the traveling sportsmen was Washington Irving, whose *Tour on the Prairies* (1835) is a convenient starting point for the long list of sportsman-chronicles that grew out of hunting expeditions in the Far West. Between 1835 and the early 1900's, printers treated the public to an unbroken series of hunting narratives, including the adventures not only of such Americans as Irving and Parkman but also of such foreign sportsmen as Ruxton, a good example of the traveling Englishman. Less numerous than the English but no less adventurous were French travelers like Auguste Nicaise, whose *Une année au désert et récits du Far-West Américain* (Chalons, 1864) recounts his adventures on a trip from Jefferson City to Walla Walla, Portland, and San Francisco in 1858 and 1859. German readers read such accounts as that written by Julius Froebel, *Aus Amerika. Erfahrungen, Reisen und Studien* (Leipzig, 1857), a record of his travels in Central America and Mexico and his adventures in the Far West in 1852, 1853, and 1854. Most of the travel journals and narratives like those named are factual, although frequently the writers peer through "the mellow moonshine of romance," as Twain puts it, and see a Noble Red Man or two.[43] But at the same time, a lush undergrowth of pseudo- and sub-factual literature of Far Western adventure flourished: Emerson Bennett's *The Trapper's Bride, or the Spirit of Adventure;* Charles A. Murray's *The Prairie Bird;* Charles W. Webber's *Old Hicks the Guide; or, Adventures in the Camanche Country in Search of a Gold Mine;* D. W. Belisle's *The American Family Robinson; or, the Adventures of a Family Lost in the Great Desert of the West;* R. Richards' *The California Crusoe; or, the Lost Treasure Found, A Tale of Mormonism;* and numerous others. In addition, Beadle and Company's first dime novel in 1860 inaugurated a new and greater epoch in Far Western romances.

One of the stock features of both the factual journal and the cheap romance was the buffalo hunt. Until about 1875, when the herds became greatly diminished, the sportsman's journal or the romance which did not feature a hunter galloping across the plains on the heels of stampeding buffalo was not taking full advantage of the available raw materials of adventure. Naturally, then, before many days of his journey have elapsed, the tenderfoot in *Roughing It* has the opportunity, fortuitously provided by a breakdown of his "mud-wagon," to hunt buffalo, and like a host of hunters before him he finds "it was noble sport galloping over the plain in the dewy freshness of the morning." The hunt ends like many a one reported in the literature under discussion. Like the legions of hunters who had fled enraged animals before him, Bemis takes shelter in the "only solitary tree ... in nine counties adjacent." Typical of such escapes are those in J. Ross Browne's *A Dangerous Journey* and Bénédict Révoil's *Shooting and Fishing in the Rivers, Prairies, and Backwoods of North America.* Browne found safety in the crotch of his tree after winning a half-mile foot race with a herd of wild longhorn cattle. Révoil found his tree about 350 miles west of San Antonio just in time to escape from a wounded bear and a war party of Comanches. Less fortunate than most tree climbers in this literature, M. Révoil found the tree already occupied by a panther.

The hunters who climbed the tree are no less remarkable than the tree itself, a fact revealed by the manner in which they extricated themselves from their predicaments. J. Ross Browne was notably uninspired because he did nothing to extricate himself. Instead his rescue from the herd of cattle milling about below his perch was effected by a grizzly bear which, with a valor totally untempered by discretion, defied the whole herd in order to attack a young bull. Fortunately enough for Browne, the bear and the bull fight until both drop dead, and the double catastrophe frightens off the remainder of the herd.[44] Révoil reports two of the most marvelous instances of the hunter *semper paratus,* both occurring on a bear hunt west of San Antonio. For illustration the first is sufficient, for it includes the famous tree, a remarkably intelligent animal, and the resourceful hunter. One of the hunting party is a small old man armed only with a spear and a brace of pistols. At the sight of the first bear, the old man, off at a gallop, soon closes the gap sufficiently to permit a spear thrust or two at the bear's hindquarters. The bear turns and attacks the pony, which promptly throws the old man in a complete somersault over his head. The old man then takes refuge in a large oak which happened to be near. The little man climbed up the tree as high as the branches could bear him, and holding on with his left hand, used the spear with his right, and kept the bear from getting up at him. To render the scene complete, the pony was capering about the foot of the tree like a mad creature, whinnying and tearing up the earth with its hoofs, as if it understood its master's peril and wished to help him out of it.[45]

One can only entertain the most amazed admiration for the presence of mind which permitted the little gentleman to retain his grasp upon his spear through the somersault from the saddle and the climb up the tree.

No evidence suggests that Twain had read either of these two particular works, although he was personally acquainted with Browne and, therefore, probably knew of his narrative. But the two books exemplify a type of fiction with which Twain certainly was familiar, for they represent the type of book upon which not only the Bemis episode but the whole of *Roughing It* is a burlesque commentary. With such literature forming the tenderfoot's conception of "noble sport," obviously an important step in his education is the correction of such notions. Appropriately the hunt ends in "disaster and disgrace," and Bemis' proofs fail to convince the two travelers of his veracity. When the tenderfoot concludes "that if this man was not a liar he only missed it by the skin of his teeth," he has advanced perceptibly toward that maturity which characterizes the old-timer.

Whether or not Twain ever actually participated in a buffalo hunt during the overland journey to Nevada must remain a matter of conjecture, but that he visited the Humboldt mining regions and indulged in some prospecting is a matter of record. Out of his visit grew the snowstorm episode in *Roughing It,* a fine burlesque of Far Western adventure as it appeared in contemporary literature. That the episode is a burlesque is quite clear the moment Mark Twain speaks of the "common book-fraud about Indians and lost hunters making a fire by rubbing two sticks together." The remark and the previous comment about making a fire with a pistol also serve to indicate the burlesque target, the same sort of literature as that forming the background of the Bemis episode. Indeed the inexhaustibly resourceful Révoil, while lost near Cape Girardeau in a snowstorm, wanders in circles until the "large number of footprints in the snow" reveals the error and saves himself with a pistol-ignited fire.[46] Twain's episode certainly burlesques this sort of hunting adventure, but like Bemis' Allen pistol it is more "comprehensive."

Aside from the explicit references to the literature burlesqued, additional evidence of the burlesque nature of the episode appears in the characterization of the tenderfoot's companion, Ballou. Although some of his traits are those of Twain's actual companion Tillou, Ballou is nevertheless a burlesque character, and his appearance complicates any discussion about the burlesque target. His chief characteristic is his "Partingtonian fashion of loving and using big words *for their own sakes,* and independent of any bearing they might have upon the thought he was purposing to convey." Twain's use of the word "Partingtonian" in this description erroneously implies a kinship between Ballou and Benjamin P. Shillaber's character. Mrs. Partington is a lineal descendant of Mrs. Malaprop; Ballou is not. When Ballou speaks of the horses as "bituminous from long deprivation," he reveals his descent, not from Mrs. Malaprop, but from the "Oracle" in *The Innocents Abroad* and from little Etna in Webb's *St. Twel'mo.* However, Ballou does not always "let his ponderous syllables fall with an easy unconsciousness that left them wholly without offensiveness." Instead he talks in such fashion only twice, on the trip to the mining region and during the snowstorm. In the interval he is a quite coherent old-timer who superintends the tenderfoot's education in prospecting. For example, no ponderous syllable falls when he summarizes the prospects for success around Unionville:

It's fair enough here, maybe, but overrated. Seven-thousand-dollar ledges are scarce, though. That Sheba may be rich enough, but we don't own it; and, besides, the rock is so full of base metals that all the science in the world can't work it. We'll not starve, here, but we'll not get rich, I'm afraid.

Even his disappointment when the tenderfoot's "piles of pure gold and silver" turn out to be fool's gold does not jar him into incoherence, although surely the provocation was just as great as that which caused him to say of Ollendorff, "he 'did not know as much as a logarithm!' "

The discrepancy in Ballou's linguistic ability is matched by a discrepancy in his lore. At Unionville, his sagacity makes him the natural guide of the party, but in the snowstorm episode he becomes as ignorant as the tenderfoot and Ollendorff, subscribing with them to the two common book-frauds. The most plausible explanation for such an inconsistency is Twain's confusion of two separate conceptions of the character. The Ballou who tutors the narrator in mining is representative of Twain's actual companion, Tillou. Ballou the incoherent is a burlesque character.

Not much is made of the burlesque Ballou at the beginning of the Humboldt narrative; his fondness for big words is explained and illustrated briefly, but almost immediately the character merges into that of Ballou the coherent, a figure maintained consistently throughout the whole episode at Unionville. The burlesque character does not figure prominently in any action until the start of the return journey, during which the narrator, Ballou, and Ollendorff are marooned by the flood, experience the tyranny of the outlaw "Arkansas," and lose their way in the snowstorm. Because the climax of the snowstorm episode depends on the death speeches of the three travelers, parodies of those of the numerous remorseful villains to be found in the religious and semi-religious writing of the period, the name of this character may conceal a reference to John Ballou, a minister and a writer of some local repute in Cincinnati, who affords some of the most nauseous death speeches in literature, particularly in his *The Lady of the West; or, the Gold Seekers,* published in Cincinnati, 1855. Other than the coincidence of names, however, no evidence in the episode connects it either with John Ballou or with the book he wrote.

Thematically, the snowstorm episode and its sequel, the backsliding of the reformed "villains" the next day, serve the same purpose as the Bemis episode. That is, they prove to the tenderfoot, now approaching maturity following his experiences at the mines, that the romantic death of a repentant sinner is not so lightly accomplished, nor is repentance itself easy. Indeed such things are as hard to attain and maintain as it is to make a fire by the methods recommended in the romances. Quite appropriately, the three "shook hands and agreed to say no more about 'reform' and 'examples to the rising generation.' "

The episode immediately preceding the snowstorm adventure is much more difficult to assess; at first glance and, indeed, after the third or fourth scrutiny, the events at "Honey Lake Smith's" defy description. The whole episode trembles on the verge of, but never clearly falls into, burlesque. But apparently Twain intended it to be a burlesque, for he uses the same device, that of scrambled geography, which he describes in his explanation of the "Bloody Massacre":

Ah, it was a deep, deep satire, and most ingeniously contrived. But I made the horrible details so carefully and conscientiously interesting that the public devoured *them* greedily, and wholly overlooked the following distinctly-stated facts, to wit: The murderer was perfectly well known to every creature in the land as a *bachelor,* and consequently he could not murder his wife and nine children; he murdered them "in his splendid dressed-stone mansion just in the edge of the great pine forest between Empire City and Dutch Nick's," when even the very pickled oysters that came on our tables knew that there was not a "dressed-stone mansion" in all Nevada Territory; also that, so far from there being a "great pine forest between Empire City and Dutch Nick's," there wasn't a solitary tree within fifteen miles of either place; and, finally, it was patent and notorious that Empire City and Dutch

Nick's were one and the same place, and contained only six houses anyhow, and consequently there could be no forest between them.[47]

The adventure begins at " 'Honey Lake Smith's,' a sort of isolated inn on the Carson river. It was a two-story log house situated on a small knoll in the midst of the vast basin or desert through which the sickly Carson winds its melancholy way." Actually, Honey Lake Smith's was not in the midst of the basin. A station on the main overland trail between Ragtown and Carson City, it stood on the eastern edge of the Twenty-Six Mile Desert on the great bend of the Carson River and marked the divergence of two well-traveled roads, one leading straight westward to Dayton on the western fringe of the desert, the other southwestward, skirting the edge of the desert and following the Carson River to Fort Churchill, thence to Dayton where it rejoins the other road. On its east-west axis, marked by the direct road from Honey Lake Smith's to Dayton, the desert is twenty-six miles long, hence its name. As one travels westward, the first seven miles of the journey take him through the widest part of the desert. Here a scant ten miles measure the distance from the range of steep hills on the north to the Carson River on the south. The remaining seventeen miles of the journey are through a trough from three to five miles wide between two ranges of precipitous hills.[48] In short, a traveler would have to work hard in order to lose himself in this area. According to Twain's account, the party left Honey Lake Smith's in the morning and two hours later found themselves back at the starting point after traveling in circles. Thus, if they made a late start, the travelers were back at Honey Lake Smith's by about 10:00 A.M. From 10:00 A.M. to 3:00 P.M. or a little later, they followed at a trot first the stagecoach itself and later its tracks in the snow. Five hours at such a gait should have brought them all the way to Carson City. But after traveling until nightfall, preparing to die, and finally backsliding from all the grand resolutions, the party finds itself at a station located "at the verge of the Twenty-Six Mile Desert." Because the station is described only as "a stage station," it obviously is not the town of Dayton upon the western edge of the desert, but must be, both from location and description, Honey Lake Smith's again, the only stage station on either verge of the desert. In other words, just as Twain inserted a great pine forest between Empire City and Dutch Nick's so has he inserted a wild, snow-filled day and night of wandering between two places which in actuality were the same. The use of such a trick suggests the existence of a burlesque intention in all the adventures associated with Honey Lake Smith's and indicates the possible fictional character of all that is said concerning the desperado "Arkansas."

The inclusion of the "Arkansas" episode in the burlesque is further suggested by Twain's comments about the snowstorms which bracket the whole section in the book. Before Twain's party arrived at the station, it "rode through a snowstorm for two or three days," traversing without difficulty four times the distance between Honey Lake Smith's and Carson through a much more desolate region. They left in another blinding snowstorm. Insofar as the weather itself is concerned Twain is fairly accurate; the 1861-62 winter was a particularly severe one with unprecedented snows on the Nevada side of the Sierra. In a letter to his wife dated January 16, 1862 (preserved in the Mark Twain Papers), Orion Clemens described a flood in Carson City, the result of a heavy but rapidly thawing snowfall, and announced that Sam, returning from Unionville, had been "water bound" for a week sixty miles to the east. But certainly exception must be taken to Twain's remark that "this was not the rainy season." Twain is separating the inseparable weather-wise just as he did in geography. The rainy season in Nevada is coincident with the period of possible snowfall, late September or October to March.

Although such deliberate inconsistencies point in the direction of burlesque or hoax in the "Arkansas" episode, it is difficult to determine whether or not literary burlesque is hidden here. Like the other burlesque episodes, it represents a further step in the tenderfoot's education by confronting him with a blowhard gunman of the sort to be found in any romance of the mining regions. As a result the tenderfoot and the reader get a pointed contrast between "Arkansas," the pseudo-desperado, and Slade, the enigmatic badman, the puzzling mixture of good and bad, of bravery and cowardice. If the episode is literary burlesque, the only fruitful clues to a specific source are the names of the two principals, "Arkansas" and Johnson. Possibly Twain had in mind the romances written by Friedrich Gerstäcker, the English versions of which were published under the pseudonym "Francis Johnson."[49] Many of the Johnson stories are laid in Arkansas; for example, the 1862 series published by Dick and Fitzgerald include *The Regulators of Arkansas, Rowson the Renegade,* and *Bill Johnson or The Outlaws of Arkansas* (actually separate sections of *Die Regulatoren von Arkansas* reprinted in translation). All his other romances feature an Arkansan or present an event in Arkansas, usually a lynching. In 1870 and 1871, when Twain was at work on *Roughing It,* "Francis Johnson" attained a new prominence by dominating the publication list of Beadle and Adams' American Tales, second series. Beginning with *The Gold Guides; or, Steel Arm, the Regulator,* issued on April 22, 1870, Beadle and Adams printed twelve Johnson tales in a total of twenty-five issues to the end of 1871.[50] Certainty is not at all possible, but, delving as he apparently did into the regions of western romance, Twain may have noticed a few Johnson tales and constructed as a burlesque the Honey Lake Smith episode featuring a man named Johnson at the mercy of a desperado named "Arkansas." But the trail is vague and the clues are slight; the tracker feels no comforting degree of assurance.

No such measure of uncertainty characterizes the *Weekly Occidental* episode, a burlesque interesting in several ways. With the exception of the novel supposedly written for the paper and of two details concerning the staff, Twain is reasonably accurate in his facts about the *Occidental*.[51] But the "dissolute stranger with a literary turn of mind" who turns up in Virginia City, joins the *Occidental* staff, and ruins the serialized novel is a fiction; the fact that the second version of his chapter is a burlesque of Charles Reade's *Love Me Little Love Me Long* identifies him as Webb, who singled out Charles Reade as his special burlesque target in *Liffith Lank, or Lunacy*. Webb, of course, visited Virginia City, but not during the lifetime of the *Occidental* because he did not arrive in California until April 20, 1864, a full month after the demise of the magazine.[52] In addition, Twain apparently has exaggerated his own role on the paper, for during the planning of the *Occidental* he was in Carson City reporting the activities of the territorial legislature.[53] Since Carson is only twenty miles from Virginia City, he certainly could have played a role as important as he implies his was, but contemporary newspaper accounts indicate that his name was not publicly associated with the paper at all.[54]

However, fact or near fact gives way to fiction the moment Twain undertakes a description of the serialized novel which proved the downfall of the paper. According to Twain, the job of writing the weekly chapter was to rotate among the various staff members, but obviously no such novel as Twain describes was ever actually attempted. Instead, Twain's chapter summaries constitute a composite burlesque of several popular English authors. The first two summaries afford such meager evidence that it is impossible to do more than guess about the burlesque targets. Mrs. F.'s "ineffable" heroine might have been created by almost any popular novelist, English or American, in the nineteenth century; but because this heroine is the creation of a woman, the target may be either Mrs. M. E. Braddon or Mrs. Henry Wood, both favorites of the burlesque writers. The summary of the second chapter affords even less evidence. That Mr. F. introduces a "brilliant lawyer" may indicate a burlesque thrust at

Anthony Trollope, whose fondness for lawyers is certainly a distinguishing characteristic, but the summary affords grounds for nothing but speculation. Mr. D.'s section, the third chapter, however, is clearly a burlesque of Bulwer-Lytton, for in this chapter the "mysterious Rosicrucian" appears. By the 1870's the Rosicrucian had become the standard means of identifying a burlesque of Bulwer-Lytton. Thackeray had established the practice in his *Novels by Eminent Hands,* and subsequent writers of burlesques in *Punch, Fun,* and the other humor magazines had followed his lead. Harte, of course, used the same device in the *Condensed Novels.* The first chapter attempted by the dissolute stranger burlesques no particular author, but succeeds in burlesquing the amazingly ingenious plot resolutions common to most "sensation" novels; the second attempt is, as Twain says, a burlesque of Charles Reade's *Love Me Little Love Me Long.*[55]

The *Occidental* novel is the only burlesque worked into the fabric of *Roughing It* not connected with the literature of the Far West. Unlike the other two episodes, it does not deflate any of the tenderfoot's romantic notions about the West. Indeed, by the time he participates in the *Occidental* novel, the narrator is no longer a tenderfoot. He has been disillusioned in every romantic notion; he has not only experienced the West, but has settled down as a resident of the West's most booming town. He has, in short, acquired most of the wisdom of Twain, the old-timer, the writer of the tale. The *Occidental* burlesque, placed at the end of the report on the flush times in Virginia City, bears upon this fact. Prior to the history of the *Occidental,* Twain tells of the lavish expenditure of money in the Sanitary Flour Sack auction, John Smith's trip to Europe, Colonel Jim's and Colonel Jack's trip to New York, and Buck Fanshaw's funeral, each story turning upon an excess of money and a dearth of sophistication. Next, two chapters devoted to "desperadoism" and rough-and-ready justice lead up to the account of Captain Blakely's summary justice. The report on the flush times culminates in the *Occidental* episode. Consequently, by placement the episode "establishes beyond cavil that the 'flush times' are at the flood," and the *Occidental's* dismal failure emphasizes the lack of sophistication of the novelists. An implication to be drawn from the narrator's failure as a novelist and poet, too, for that matter, is that, although he once read and loved books bathed in the "mellow moonshine of romance," he now is totally incapable of writing anything of the sort. In effect, the episode becomes an implicit commentary upon the work which contains it—that is, upon *Roughing It,* which becomes by contrast the antithesis of romance.

Despite the hastily added Sandwich Islands section and the various insertions from newspaper articles and source books introduced as padding to fill out the required two volumes, *Roughing It* then exhibits a high level of craftsmanship, not only in the handling of the point of view, but also in the subordination of pure burlesque to the characterization of the protagonist, the tenderfoot traveler. The difficulty experienced in identifying specific burlesque targets in the various episodes is in itself an index to the successful assimilation of burlesque into the narrative of the tenderfoot's adventures and the chronicle of his growth. The subordination of burlesque to the new purpose indicates Twain's emergence from his burlesque apprenticeship.

The results of the endeavor between 1866 and 1871 are of considerable importance, not only because they serve as an index to Twain's craftmanship but also because they furnished the basis for further structural experiments in the major novels of the period under consideration. Starting during the apprenticeship with the character-axis of the Syntax-derived travel-burlesques and the principle of alternation between fiction and fact, Twain evolved a new and distinctive structural pattern, which is organic in the highest sense, growing naturally from the narrator's self-characterization. In his fullest development, that is, as the tenderfoot of *Roughing It,* the narrator is a traveler whose prevision of the impending journey, based upon his reading, constitutes the head of the narrative-plank. The account of the journey, the narrative-plank itself, is both a burlesque commentary upon the literature the narrator has read and a record of his education. To depict the education, Twain alternated the fiction, the book-inspired expectations of the narrator, and the disillusioning fact, the "actual" events of the journey. Because the focus of attention is no longer upon the regions traversed but upon the developing maturity of the traveler, his progress from ignorance to knowledge, from tenderfoot to old-timer, the resultant narrative cannot be called a travel-burlesque. Although it includes much burlesque and deals with a journey, it more nearly resembles a novel, if one must classify it at all.

V

Insofar as the development of structural principles is concerned, *Roughing It* is the culmination of Mark Twain's growth in the travel-narrative form. The three remaining narratives of the period we are considering, "Old Times on the Mississippi," *A Tramp Abroad,* and the last forty chapters of *Life on the Mississippi,* reveal no further advances. In "Old Times" Twain employed the same structural principles he had used in *Roughing It,* but with a greater technical mastery. The last two show a marked reversion to structural stages antedating *Roughing It* and indicate the extent to which Twain had come to rely upon the structural patterns already worked out in the earlier narratives.

The one thing Twain most successfully communicates to the reader in *A Tramp Abroad* is his own lack of ardor for the book he had contracted to write. Even if Twain's explicit testimony were lacking, the perfunctory dredging in past burlesques would amply betray his attitude toward his task. His distaste is unmistakable in his letter to Howells, written from Italy in 1878, in which he declares with vehemence his hatred for all concerned with his trip, travel, hotels, the opera, the old masters: he can only "curse" and "foam at the mouth."[56]

When he lost his Swiss notebook, he tried to use the loss as an excuse to withdraw from his contract, but the notebook turned up, and he wrote Twichell, "I went solidly to work, tore up a great part of the MS. written in Heidelberg—wrote and tore up, continued to write and tear up—and at last, reward of patient and noble persistence, my pen got the old swing again!"[57] Despite the optimistic tone of the last clause, he continued to have trouble with his book. From Paris, on March 6, 1879, he wrote Mrs. Fairbanks, "I've been having a dismal time for months over this confounded book, working hard everytime I got a chance, & tearing up a lot of the MS next time I came to read it over."[58]

Almost a full year after his optimistic letter to Twichell, he was still struggling to make something of his material, for he again writes to Twichell,

I am revising my MS. I did not expect to like it, but I do. I have been knocking out early chapters for more than a year now, not because they had no merit, but merely because they hindered the flow of the narrative; it was a dredging process. Day before yesterday my shovel fetched up three more chapters and laid them, reeking, on the festering shore-pile of their predecessors.[59]

Obviously a process of revision which is going on a year after it began and which still involves the deletion of whole chapters denies the existence of a pen with the "old swing again." The fact of the matter is that with the exception of a few episodes, the pen never did regain its swing in this book. Devoid of enthusiasm for his task, Twain lacked the incentive to produce a work comparable to *Roughing It*. Instead he produced a patchwork composed of burlesque devices which had, through frequent use, become almost second nature to him.

The source of Twain's problem with *A Tramp Abroad* was his attitude; the nature of the problem, as the last-quoted letter to Twichell indicates, was structural; clearly his manuscript lacked unity especially in the early portions, if for an entire year he had been discarding early chapters because "they hindered the flow of the narrative." The narrative pattern for which Twain shows such solicitude is quite comparable to those of the Sandwich Islands and *Quaker City* letters. It represents, then, a long stride backward, in technique at least, from the achievements of *Roughing It*. In two short paragraphs on the very first page of the narrative, Twain establishes a derivative of the character-axis basic to the nineteenth-century travel-burlesques in the Dr. Syntax tradition:

> I looked about me for the right sort of person to accompany me in the capacity of agent, and finally hired a Mr. Harris for this service.
> It was also my purpose to study art while in Europe. Mr. Harris was in sympathy with me in this. He was as much of an enthusiast in art as I was, and not less anxious to learn to paint. I desired to learn the German language; so did Harris.

Here are the artistic traveler and a companion ready for another tour of Europe. The reader's expectations, thus aroused, are not disappointed; with but few exceptions *A Tramp Abroad* is a typical outgrowth of the Dr. Syntax tours. By 1879 Twain had come nearly full circle in his travel narratives, returning almost precisely to his starting point in the Sandwich Islands letters of 1866.

Although the narrator of *A Tramp Abroad* appears in the opening paragraphs as an artistic traveler, Twain conceived of him as both artist and scientist. In the first part of the book, however, he rather ineptly concentrated upon the narrator as artist, while in the remainder he emphasized the scientific aspect. Consequently the book falls into two distinct sections. From the opening chapter to the ascent of the Riffleberg, the artistic traveler dominates the fiction. Only once in the first section does the narrator appear as a scientist; at the opening of the dueling descriptions, he writes, "One day in the interest of science my agent obtained permission to bring me to the students' dueling place." With this one exception, he is the artist traveling through Germany with his sketchbook in hand, preserving for his readers memorable scenes which he reproduces from time to time, each reproduction, in itself a graphic "burlesque" of sketches by tourists, accompanied by a critical disquisition upon his art. A good example is his sketch of the military tower in Wimpfen, about which he says,

I made a little sketch of it. I kept a copy, but gave the original to the Burgomaster. I think the original was better than the copy, because it had more windows in it and the grass stood up better and had a brisker look. There was none around the tower, though; I composed the grass myself, from studies I made in a field in Heidelberg in Hämmerling's time. The man on top, looking at the view, is apparently too large; but I found he could not be made smaller, conveniently. I wanted him there, and I wanted him visible, so I thought out a way to manage it; I composed the picture from two points of view; the spectator is to observe the man from about where that flag is, and he must observe the tower itself from the ground. This harmonizes the seeming discrepancy.

The "critical" discussion of the sketch is interesting not only because it illustrates the artistic acumen of the narrator, but also because, in the confession about the grass, it returns to the old travel-burlesque joke about the artist's right or, as Dr. Syntax puts it, "duty" to "put things in, or leave them out." When the traveler and his companion begin the ascent of the Riffleberg, Twain's conception of his narrator shifts abruptly: the narrator becomes a scientist and as such dominates the remainder of the book, although the artist intrudes once with a sketch of the Lion of St. Mark.

Side by side with these two conceptions of the narrator is another, the narrator as a serious spokesman for Twain in the factual sections of the book. The narrator's role as part-time reporter introduces the sort of inconsistency characteristic of *The Innocents Abroad.* For example, the artist almost vehemently declares his ability to recognize art despite the greatest of difficulties when he discusses Turner's "Slave Ship." As a result of his recently acquired cultivation, he claims to see realistic representations and natural effects in "glaring yellow mud" and "lurid explosions of smoke and flame." The humor of the passage depends upon the fact that the artist is incapable of appreciating art, a fact revealed by the words he uses. All his claims to the contrary, he still sees the "glaring yellow mud" and other monstrosities. The narrator as reporter discusses the very same problem in art during the return visit to Venice where once again he studies the Old Masters and wonders what it is people see in them. In asking an artist this question, he points out exactly the same defects in the Old Masters which the artistic narrator had seen in the Turner; after listening to the reply, however, he reaches quite a different conclusion: he is prepared to grant the defects while still believing there is "a something that is divine and unapproachable about the Old Master, and that there is no arguing the fact away by any system of reasoning whatever."

The traveling companion, Harris, represents the greatest departure from the earlier pattern. The usual companion, a most reluctant pupil, is not interested in the improvement of his mind and tastes. But Harris accompanies the narrator in order to study art and the German language. In fact, he becomes angry when the narrator's carelessness deprives him of an opportunity to gain more culture. When the party sleeps through the grandeurs of Meiringen, Harris' reaction is quite untypical:

I woke up the agent and gave him a piece of my mind. Instead of being humiliated, he only upbraided me for being so wanting in vigilance. He said he had expected to improve his mind by coming to Europe, but a man might travel to the ends of the earth with me and never see anything, for I was manifestly endowed with the very genius of ill luck.

The modification in the characterization of the traveling companion results from the fact that the conception of Harris is based in part upon Twain's actual companion, Joseph Twichell. Consequently, Harris is not only more interested in improvement but also is occasionally more refined than the refined traveler. For example, the narrator's supposed social blunders when he accosts a pretty young lady in the Schweitzerhof dining room cause Harris agonies of mortification. He breaks out, "Ah, me, you struck the summit! You struck the loftiest altitude of stupidity that human effort has ever reached. You shall have a monument of jackasses' skulls as high as the Strasburg spire if you die before I do." The entire episode is a complete reversal of the relationship existing between Mr. Twain and Mr. Brown of the Sandwich Islands tour. Similarly, Harris generally shows in his speech a grammatical correctness totally foreign to such a companion as Brown; in fact, at one stage of the journey he talks about the "slovenly habit of doubling up... 'have's' " with a linguistic sensitivity that lifts him well beyond the level of a Brown.

As might be expected in view of the almost total reversion to the character-axis of the Sandwich Islands and *Quaker City* letters, Twain uses almost every other device he had previously used with success, but with a craftsmanship well below that exhibited in *Roughing It.* The same alternation between the serious and the comic is here, the comic material ranging from Jim Baker's blue-jay yarn to literary burlesque; but if the reader gives any weight at all to Twain's comment about the Gambetta duel in the letter to Mrs. Fairbanks quoted earlier, he is led to expect of these humorous and burlesque episodes a level of integration actually not present. In the case of the duels, a contrast does exist betwen the factual episode and the following fiction, for Twain is reversing the common concept of student duels, that they are "very farcical affairs," by presenting the college duels in all their bloody seriousness and following the description with an adult duel reduced to a farce. The device, however, is not very effective; the comment is almost too silent and not eloquent enough.

The two burlesque episodes included in the book have not even this slender thematic connection with what precedes or follows. Like those used in *The Innocents Abroad,* they are appropriate to the setting, but otherwise they are merely burlesques within the burlesque. Of the two, the "Legend of the 'Spectacular Ruin'" is the more interesting, not only because it burlesques the sort of legend Twain has in other places introduced into the text but also because, as an allegory depicting the superiority of science over superstition, it foreshadows *A Connecticut Yankee in King Arthur's Court*. The hero of the legend is Sir Wissenschaft, "a poor and obscure knight, out of a far county." Although "science was despised in those days," Sir Wissenschaft in his ragged armor is unruffled by the jeers of the crowd when he offers to destroy the ravaging dragon. "He said he might be a little in advance of his age, but no matter,—science would come to be honored, some time or other." With his fire extinguisher, he conquers the dragon, in the context almost an allegorical symbol for error, superstition, or prejudice, because "this man had brought brains to his aid." For his reward, he claims a monopoly upon the manufacture and sale of spectacles in Germany. The monopoly had previously been abused, but the man of science is also an enlightened capitalist: "To everybody's surprise, the unselfish monopolist immediately reduced the price of spectacles to such a degree that a great and crushing burden was removed from the nation." The legend thus becomes a curious hybrid, at once a literary burlesque upon Rhine legends and a serious allegorical commentary upon the value of science. It is *A Connecticut Yankee* in miniature with one significant difference: Sir Wissenschaft conquers the dragon and brings the benefits of science to the people; Sir Boss achieves only a temporary victory—the dragon wins eventually.

The second episode, the "Skeleton for Black Forest Novel," probably should not be called a burlesque at all. Twain's references to the "Black Forest stories" suggest a connection between this "novel" and Berthold Auerbach's *Schwarzwälder Dorfgeschichten* which were quite popular both in Germany and elsewhere during the latter half of the nineteenth century.[60] But the "novel" itself has little to do with any of Auerbach's works; instead it is more closely allied to nineteenth-century theatrical melodrama. Not only does it have the typical hero, heroine, and villain and inserted stage directions, but it is also divided into the equivalent of three acts. Thus, if it is to be called a burlesque at all, it must be called a burlesque of stage melodrama, not of Auerbach's Black Forest novels.

In other respects the book is a medley of old burlesque devices. Twain's old friend, the "Oracle" of *The Innocents Abroad,* appears once again in the guise of the talkative young American on the Lake Lucerne steamer. He has changed his age and appearance, but he shows the same ability to scramble history and to cite mysterious authorities for his information: "Hi, there's Mount Pilatus coming in sight again. Named after Pontius Pilate, you know, that shot the apple off of William Tell's head. Guide-book tells all about it, they say. I didn't read it—an American told me." And once again, Twain makes use of the Webbian device of scrambled sesquipedalianism, the device he had used with Ballou in *Roughing It.* In the legend of "The Cave of the Specter," the device takes the same form it had taken in the Legend of Count Luigi in *The Innocents Abroad,* that is, scrambled medieval terms: "the von Berlichingen of that day shut his daughter up in his donjon keep, or his oubliette, or his culverin, or some such place." Harris uses a new form of the device in his "Official Report of a Visit to the Furka Region." The report is well sprinkled with pseudo-words supposed to be from Choctaw, Eskimo, Fiji, Zulu, and Chinese as well as legitimate words from French and German. This version of the device derives ultimately from the pseudo-Irish used by Webb in *Arrah-no-Poke* and by Harte in *Muck-a-Muck,* but the immediate suggestion most probably came from the mottoes prefixed to the chapters of *The Gilded Age.* Reaching deep into his past, Twain uses in his description of the waitresses at the Jungfrau Hotel a form of the device he had not repeated since he wrote "The Pioneer Ball" for the *Territorial Enterprise* back in 1865:

The table d'hôte was served by waitresses dressed in the quaint and comely costume of the Swiss peasants. This consists of a simple gros de laine, trimmed with ashes of roses, with overskirt of sacre bleu ventre saint gris, cut bias on the off side, with facings of petit polonaise and narrow insertions of pâté de foie gras backstitched to the mis en scène in the form of a jeu d'esprit. It gives to the wearer a singularly piquant and alluring aspect.

The same device appears in the narrator's scientific theory about the altitude of the moon, but this time it takes the form which Webb used with little Etna in *St. Twel'mo*, that is, a pseudo-scientific jargon:

I had a theory that the gravitation of refraction, being subsidiary to atmospheric compensation, the refrangibility of the earth's surface would emphasize this effect in regions where great mountain ranges occur, and possibly so even-handedly impact the odic and idyllic forces together, the one upon the other, as to prevent the moon from rising higher than 12,200 feet above sea level.

A Tramp Abroad shows that the travel-burlesque devices with which Twain had become familiar during his apprenticeship formed a crutch upon which he leaned heavily when he did not have the ambition or interest to attempt new things. The various letters, to Mrs. Fairbanks, Twichell, and Howells, indicate that, in the case of *A Tramp Abroad,* he took some time even to find his crutch. The mass deletions of which he speaks were made "merely because they hindered the flow of the narrative." Thus, Twain apparently took well over a year to decide that the travel-burlesque plot formed by the narrator-Harris axis should be the unifying element, and that all which "hindered" its "flow" should be cut.

VI

When Twain undertook to turn "Old Times" into a volume for the subscription trade, he was not so slow in preparing the crutch in the narrative material which he added. To the *Atlantic* articles

(Chapters IV to XVIII) he prefixed three introductory chapters, completed the "Old Times" material with the *Pennsylvania* episodes (Chapters XVIII to XX), and in a morganatic union with the product added the account of his 1882 trip. The crutch appears in the very first paragraph of Chapter XXII: "After twenty-one years' absence I felt a very strong desire to see the river again, and the steamboats, and such of the boys as might be left; so I resolved to go out there. I enlisted a poet for company, and a stenographer to 'take him down,' and started westward about the middle of April." On the actual trip, Twain was accompanied by Osgood and a stenographer; in the narrative, Osgood becomes the poet, his transformation establishing a character-axis similar to that of *A Tramp Abroad.*

In the subsequent paragraphs of the chapter, the narrator emerges as an amalgam of Twain, the knowledgeable veteran of river-piloting, and the familiar Syntax-type traveler. At the outset, a certain level of refinement may be assumed in a man who chooses a poet for a companion. Furthermore, like Dr. Syntax, he is searching for something curious to enter in his notebook. To this end he decides to disguise himself and the members of his party, because he "remembered that it was the custom of steamboat-men in the old times to load up the confiding stranger with the most picturesque and admirable lies, and put the sophisticated friend off with dull and ineffectual facts." However, in his search for "picturesque and admirable lies," he differs from Dr. Syntax in that he is wise enough to recognize a lie; Dr. Syntax is not. Like the refined traveler, he is educated and, in contrast to the provincialism of the hinterland, urbane, at least in the matter of dress. The first quotation from the narrator's notebook is *"Evening*—Speaking of dress. Grace and picturesqueness drop gradually out of it as one travels away from New York." In the following comment he says, "There are plenty of ladies and gentlemen in the provincial cities whose garments are all made by the best tailors and dressmakers of New York; yet this has no perceptible effect upon the grand fact: the educated eye never mistakes those people for New-Yorkers." To complete the catalogue of characteristics derived from Twain's experience in travel-burlesque, the narrator is a scientific observer; his notebook entry for the afternoon of April 19 reads, "At the railway stations the loafers carry *both* hands in their breeches pockets; it was observable, heretofore that one hand was sometimes out-of-doors—here, never. This is an important fact in geography."

The added material is not great literature: some of it is interesting, some of it quite humorous, and some quite dull. As Kenneth Andrews says, *"Life on the Mississippi* is one-third magnificence and two-thirds the hack work of a professional traveler."[61] But, although the book is two-thirds hack work, it escapes being two-thirds the hack work of a professional writer of travel-burlesque. To this degree at least, it is superior to *A Tramp Abroad.* Though the last forty chapters are a heterogeneous compilation, Twain's interest in his subject was such that they were written with an enthusiasm totally lacking in much of *A Tramp Abroad;* consequently he rarely needed his crutch. In fact, the character-axis prepared in Chapter XXII figures prominently only in the episode detailing the narrator's mission to Napoleon, Arkansas, in response to Karl Ritter's dying request.

When the enthusiasm engendered by the revisiting of familiar stretches of the river does wane, he fails to use the fiction he has prepared. Instead he ends the book with a series of burlesques connected with the other matter of the book, as in *The Innocents Abroad,* only by virtue of their appropriateness to the setting. His interest in his subject is fairly obvious until his chronicle takes him northward from Keokuk. At this point in the book, he inserts one more or less factual chapter dealing with the upper river between Keokuk and La Crosse and then, in the next chapter, plunges into burlesque. The remaining two chapters, Chapters LIX and LX, take their inspiration from the literature Twain has read in preparation for the writing of his book. Much of the exposition is little more than a padding of the list of steamboat landings in the guidebook. Two of the legends, "Peboan and Seegwun" and "The Undying Head," are borrowed, with acknowledgment, from Henry R. Schoolcraft's *The Myth of Hiawatha and Other Oral Legends, Mythologic and Allegoric, of the North American Indians.*[62]

Twain's burlesque legend, "A Legend of White-Bear Lake" is no more than a mediocre burlesque which Twain makes worse with a labored analysis of his own invention. Typically, he chooses to complain about the obscure business of the two trees and the fate of the blanket, leaving the reader to notice such obvious absurdities as the bright moon in "the bright blue heavens" and the maiden's name, Kis-se-me-pa, that is, "Kiss me, pa." The disheartened reader is inclined to regret that Twain did not end the book at least a chapter sooner.

The tediousness of the burlesque legend stands out the more against the parody and burlesque which appear in Chapter LIX when the old gentleman from La Crosse boards the steamer. The old gentleman begins an elaborately rhetorical discourse about the scenery of the upper river, filling his descriptions with such "fine surprises of lurid eloquence at such judicious intervals" that the narrator correctly surmises he has traveled with a panorama. The old panoramist's speech, studded with picturesque descriptions and graced with one burlesque legend, is a burlesque and parody of an article entitled "Sketches on the Upper Mississippi" published in *Harper's* in 1853. Twain found his way to the *Harper's* article from the guidebook he used during his trip on the upper river, John Disturnell's *Sailing on the Great Lakes and Rivers of America,*[63] from which he borrowed with only four minor changes the passage concerning the "sublime Maiden's Rock":

"And so we glide along: in due time encountering those majestic domes, the mighty Sugar Loaf, and the sublime Maiden's Rock—which latter, romantic superstition has invested with a voice; and ofttimes as the birch canoe glides near, at twilight, the dusky paddler fancies he hears the soft music of the long-departed Winona, darling of Indian song and story."[64]

In Disturnell's guidebook the passage concludes the legend of Winona: "Superstition invests that rock with a voice; and oftentimes, as the birch canoe glides near it at twilight, the dusky paddler fancies he hears the soft, low music of the dirge of Winona."[65] Disturnell's acknowledgment of his source, "Copied from Harper's Magazine, July, 1853," led Twain to the original article which in turn became the target for the burlesque which precedes and follows the mention of Maiden's Rock.

Using the alliterative and rhythmic style learned from Webb, Twain aims his burlesque almost exclusively at the picturesque descriptions in the original, a fact made clear by the old panoramist's reference to the requisites of a good picturesque description: "And then the monstrous bluffs on both sides of the river—ragged, rugged, dark-complected—just the frame that's wanted; you always want a strong frame, you know, to throw up the nice points of a delicate picture and make them stand out." The principal device of the burlesque is a syntactical ambiguity, dependent upon vague pronoun references or postposed modifiers, principally participial or prepositional phrases inserted between the major elements of the sentence pattern. The result is a series of bewildering and ludicrous statements:

"And next we glide through silver waters, amid lovely and stupendous aspects of nature that attune our hearts to adoring admiration, about twelve miles, and strike Mount Vernon, six hundred feet high, with romantic ruins of a once first-class hotel perched far among the cloud shadows that mottle its dizzy heights."

In addition to the general burlesque, Twain parodies one particular paragraph describing the scenery above Prairie Du Crosse, which in the original reads,

After leaving Prairie Du Crosse, the scenery changed from the mere beautiful and picturesque to an aspect of grandeur. On each side of the river arose lofty bluffs—some rocky, and some alluvial—presenting the appearance of Cyclopean towers, grand old castles in ruins, and grotesque figures of undefinable shape. These cliffs rise to an altitude sometimes of six hundred feet; and being highly colored by the variety of materials of which they are composed, crowned often with lofty pines, and clumps of birch and chestnut-trees, and hidden below by dense forests of oak, they have a mysterious beauty and magnificence hardly to be described.[66]

No single device governs the parody; instead Twain uses a variety of methods to reduce the passage from the sublime to the ridiculous. The "grand old castles in ruins" of the original are reduced in the speech of the old panoramist to "romantic ruins of a once first-class hotel." Although the awe-inspired author of the original found the wooded cliffs "grotesque figures of undefinable shape," the panoramist exhaustively specifies the shape of his: "Our attention is attracted by a most striking promontory rising over five hundred feet—the ideal mountain pyramid. Its conic shape, thickly wooded surface girding its sides, and its apex like that of a cone, cause the spectator to wonder at nature's working." The figurative "Cyclopean tower" of the original literally becomes one in the panoramist's description: "From its dizzy heights superb views of the forests, streams, bluffs, hills, and dales, below and beyond for miles are brought within its focus."

The old gentleman's whole discourse on the scenery of the upper Mississippi is one of the best burlesques of picturesque description Twain ever wrote, and it is insofar as burlesque is concerned the only bright spot in the entire addition of 1882. In general structure the addition with which Twain supplemented the *Atlantic* articles shows only vestiges of the travel-burlesque structure which he inherited from his fellow Bohemians in San Francisco, the structure with which he had experimented and from which he had evolved the achievement of *Roughing It*. Only one travel book follows *Life on the Mississippi: Following the Equator,* published fourteen years later in 1897, a travel journal, not a travel narrative, for here the vestiges are gone. Even the fictive narrator is almost totally effaced by the man himself, Samuel L. Clemens. Consequently, *Life on the Mississippi,* published in 1883, completes the

cycle of experimentation which began in 1866 with the Sandwich
Islands letters. The fruitful portion of the cycle is the period from
1866 to 1871, from the Sandwich Islands letters to *Roughing It,*
a period characterized by a markedly conscious and successful
endeavor to mold and modify the inherited travel-burlesque devices
to meet the demands of Twain's purpose. The abrupt decline from
the peak reached with *Roughing It* clearly marks the last two
travel narratives of this period as pot-boilers; after *Roughing It*
Twain's interest shifted to the novel, where he continued his
structural experiments.

4

The Craft of the Novel

AFTER 1871, when Mark Twain shifted his attention from the travel narrative to the novel, he encountered a structural problem he had never faced before: the invention of a frame or narrative-plank, a plot which would govern the sequence of events in his book and guide it to a proper conclusion. In the travel narratives the invention of such a plot was unnecessary. The Mr. Twain–Mr. Brown character-axis and its several modifications conjoined with the itinerary of an actual journey automatically ordered his narrative. The character-axis as narrative-plank provided the frame for a succession of comic-serious contrasts, and the itinerary dictated the sequence of events from the beginning to the end of the journey. Freed of all worries about total structure, Twain was able to concentrate his efforts upon the proper disposition of the fictive elements in relation to the actual events of the journey. The novel furnishes no such ready-made outline: even the frame must be created.

In a sense, the new problem was the reverse of the one Twain had faced as a neophyte writer of travel-burlesques. When he began the Sandwich Islands series, he was equipped with a fiction, the character-axis, and confronted with the necessity of inserting the facts of his journey into the fiction. When he undertook the writing of a novel, he was equipped with a fund of memories, observations, and experiences, too heterogeneous to permit the formation of a unified whole with them alone, and confronted with the necessity of finding a fiction into which he could insert some or all of his factual material. Apparently influenced in his conception of a novel by his Hartford associates or by those novels he had read (and burlesqued during his apprenticeship), he did not immediately realize that he had already developed in *Roughing It* a suitable structural pattern—one which, with but few modifications, was to furnish the structure of his greatest novel, *Huckleberry Finn*. Thus, in the early novels of his own construction, *Tom Sawyer* and *The Prince and the Pauper*, he sought the solution to the problem of total structure not in his travel narratives but among his condensed-burlesque novels, although he readily enough employed other devices already perfected in the travel narratives in meeting internal structural problems.

The first full-length novel with which Twain was concerned was *The Gilded Age*, written in collaboration with Charles Dudley Warner in 1873. Ernest E. Leisy has explored the collaboration to discover which sections of the final text were actually written by Warner and which by Twain.[1] But, despite this information, to learn what ideas concerning the form of the novel were Mark Twain's own is impossible. Behind each contribution actually written by Twain or Warner were planning sessions in which the two exchanged ideas and proposals about the course of events in the novel. Warner testifies to the fact in a letter to Whitelaw Reid, April 7, 1873: "We have hatched the plot day by day, drawn out the characters and written it so that we cannot exactly say which belongs to who; though the different styles will show in the chapters."[2] A further insight into the methods employed by the collaborators comes from Twain's letter to Mrs. Fairbanks, April 16, 1873:

Three more chapters will end the book. I laid out the plan of the *boss* chapter, the climax chapter, yesterday, & Warner will write it up to-day; I wrote it up yesterday, & shall work & trim & polish at it to-day—& to-night we shall read, & the man who has written it best is all right —the other man's MS. will be torn up. If *neither* succeeds, we'll both write the chapter over again.[3]

At least once, an idea originated by Twain was entrusted to Warner but, after Warner's failure, was finally put into words by Twain. On April 26, 1873, Twain wrote to Livy:

> Warner failed on his description of Laura as a school-girl—as a *picture* of her, I mean. He had simply copied Miss Woolson's pretty description almost word for word—the plagiarism would have been detected in a moment. I told him so—he saw it & yet I'm hanged if he didn't hate to lose it because there was a "nip" & a pungency about that woman's phrases that he hated to lose—& so did I, only they weren't ours & we couldn't take them. So I set him to create a picture & he went at it. I finally took paper & pencil, had a thought, (as to phraseology) & scratched it down. I had already told him what the *details* of the picture should be, & so only choice language was needed to dress them in. Then we read our two efforts, & mine being rather the best, we used it. And so it *ought* to have been the best. If I had been trying to describe a picture that was in *his* mind, I would have botched it.[4]

Because this letter follows by ten days Twain's announcement of the *"boss"* chapter, it indicates that even in the process of revision the mingling of ideas and efforts continued.[5] These letters make it fairly obvious that without an explicit statement on the matter one has no way of knowing which author was responsible for an idea finally incorporated in the novel. *The Gilded Age,* then, supplies no reliable information about Mark Twain's ideas of structure.

I

Tom Sawyer, published in 1876, furnishes the first clear evidence of Twain's use of an early condensed burlesque, "The Boy's Manuscript," to provide the structure of a full-length novel. Ever since its publication in Bernard DeVoto's *Mark Twain at Work,* "The Boy's Manuscript" (c. 1870) has been recognized as the seed from which *Tom Sawyer* grew, but the nature of the seed and the process of growth have not yet been fully and carefully explored. DeVoto is willing to grant the importance of the sketch because it is the first use Twain made of the Hannibal material, but he finds it "crude and trivial, false in sentiment, clumsily farcical, an experiment in burlesque with all its standards mixed."[6] As a burlesque "The Boy's Manuscript" is not as bad as DeVoto paints it; the mistake in judgment springs from the application to the burlesque of critical standards appropriate to *Tom Sawyer;* DeVoto forgets that the primary purpose of a burlesque is not to present a boyhood idyl but to capitalize upon the absurdities of the target.

That Twain should rummage among his early burlesque novels seeking aid in the construction of *Tom Sawyer* is not at all surprising, for during the last three years of his burlesque apprenticeship— that is, from 1868 to 1870—he began experimenting with the condensed novel, attempting to find not only an escape from the limitations of the form but also an entry into original plots and themes of his own. The first attempt, "The Story of Mamie Grant, The Child Missionary," although never published, is the best of Mark Twain's condensed-novel burlesques. While visiting her aunt and uncle Mamie receives a series of callers one day in the absence of her aunt: the census-taker come to collect the taxes, the paperboy seeking his money, a man wishing to repay a $1,000 loan to her uncle, and the mortgagor asking for the $1,000 due on the house. An habitué of Sunday schools and an avid reader of religious tracts, Mamie meets each caller at the door, a tract in her hand, a sermon on her lips; as a result, each caller flees without accomplishing his mission. By evening, her uncle is completely ruined, his property attached and his family faced with eviction, but Mamie is satisfied.

In each interview Mamie summarizes the contents of the tract she is pressing into the caller's hand, each summary constituting in actuality a condensed burlesque of religious tracts. She has a number of such pamphlets: "The Doomed Drunkard, or the Wages of Sin," "Deuces or the Gamester's Last Throw," "James Wilson, the Boy Missionary," "Fire and Brimstone or the Sinner's Last Gasp," "The Slave of Gain or the Dirge of the Damned," "The Blasphemous Sailor Awfully Rebuked," and "William Baxter, the Reformed Inebriate, or, Saved as by Fire." The last two, among those summarized, serve to illustrate a new strength in Mark Twain's use of burlesque. In "The Blasphemous Sailor Awfully Rebuked," Mamie uses a pseudo-nautical gibberish:

It tells how, on a stormy night, a wicked sailor was ordered to ascend to the main hatch and reef a gasket in the sheet anchor; from his dizzy height he saw the main-tops'l jib-boom fetch away from the clew-garnets of the booby-hatch; next the leascuppers of the mizzen-to'gallants'l fouled with the peak-halliards of the cat-heads, yet in his uncurbed iniquity, at such a time as this he raised his blasphemous voice and shouted an oath in the teeth of the raging winds. Mark the quick retribution. The weather-brace parted amidships, the mizzen-shrouds fouled the starboard gang-way, and the dog-watch whipped clean out of the bolt-ropes quicker than the lightning's flash![7]

The device is not new; Twain first used it in the Sandwich Islands letters, but it gains new point from Mamie's apology which follows the summary: "I do not know what those dreadful nautical terms mean, for I am not educated & deeply learned in the matters of practical everyday life like the gifted theological students, who have learned all about practical life from the writings of other theological students who went before them." By putting the apology in the mouth of Mamie Grant, Twain gives his burlesque a double dimension and, as a consequence, a forceful and stinging irony.

In a similar fashion, he gains additional force in the burlesque summary of "William Baxter, the Reformed Inebriate, or, Saved as by Fire." In a drunken rage, Baxter kills his wife and children; shocked by his deed, he repents, reforms, marries, and soon becomes a drunkard again. A second time he kills his wife and children in a drunken rage, and once again he repents and reforms, but with the same result. The third time, after slaying his latest crop of babes with a junk bottle and throwing the "wife of his bosom" from the third-story window,

he woke from his drunken stupor to find himself alone in the world, a hopeless, friendless outcast. Be warned, be warned by his experience. But see what perseverance may accomplish. Thoroughly reformed at

last, he now traverses the land a brand plucked from the burning,
& delivers temperance lectures & organizes Sunday Schools.

As the mortgagor, her victim in this interview, hurries away from
the door, Mamie calls after him the culminating absurdity: "Go
thou & do likewise." The same irony exists, of course, on a larger
scale, in the major plot itself, for Mamie is completely unconscious
of the fact that her reforming zeal has resulted not in a better world,
but in the ruin of her uncle. As she goes to sleep, she says, "I have
saved a paper carrier, a census bureau, a creditor & a debtor, & they
will bless me forever. I have done a noble work today. I may yet
see my poor little name in a beautiful Sunday school book & maybe
T. S. Arthur may write it. Oh, joy!"

In a study of structure, "Mamie Grant," written in 1868, is of
interest because it represents Mark Twain's earliest attempt to escape
the limitations of the condensed-novel form and presages much of
his later structural technique. By characterizing Mamie as one who
without reservation accepts all she reads as a guide for her own
conduct, Twain transforms her story into a frame for a number of
additional burlesques. Thus the major plot of "Mamie Grant" is
analogous to the narrative-plank of the travel narratives, and Mamie
foreshadows not only the tenderfoot traveler of *Roughing It* but
also Tom Sawyer and to some extent Tom Canty and Huckleberry
Finn. Like Mamie, all these characters to varying degrees (Huck to
the slightest extent of all) permit their reading or their book-derived
notions to mold their concept of observable reality within the fictive
world and consequently furnish Twain the opportunity to include
literary burlesque within the framework of his major plot. Mamie
is, then, the first manifestation of an important structural device.

A different and a much simpler sort of experimentation is seen
in two other pieces written at the end of the 1860's: the "Legend of
the Capitoline Venus," published in the *Buffalo Express,* October 23,
1869, and the "Awful, Terrible Medieval Romance," published in
the *Buffalo Express,* January 1, 1870. Both stories are in the typical

condensed-novel form, but neither is a true burlesque. Although the plot of each depends to a great extent upon situations and devices common to much of the contemporary literature which Twain frequently burlesqued, the humor does not derive from the reflection of such literature in the story. Instead, Mark Twain uses a form previously reserved for burlesque to give structure to humorous ideas which formerly would have emerged as sketches or anecdotes.

Tom Sawyer is the result of a more successful attempt to use a burlesque novel as the basis of a longer work of fiction and as the vehicle for some of Twain's own humorous ideas. The positive identification of the specific target of "The Boy's Manuscript," if indeed there is any, is probably not possible, partly because the burlesque is a fragment, the first two pages being lost. Mark Twain, like the other practitioners of the art of burlesque, usually concentrated the key clues to the identity of the target in the title and first two or three paragraphs of the burlesque. But clearly the fragment deals with an adult courtship made ridiculous by reducing the principals to children. The courtship is already in progress: Billy Rogers has placed an apple where his beloved can find it and is rehearsing his speech, a burlesque of the effusions typical of the nineteenth-century literary courtship:

First I thought I would call her Dear Amy, though I was a little afraid; but soon I got used to it and it was beautiful. Then I changed it to Sweet Amy—which was better—and then I changed it again, to Darling Amy—which was bliss. When I got it all fixed at last, I was going to say, "Darling Amy, if you found an apple on the doorstep, which I think you did find one there, it was *me* that done it, and I hope you'll think of me sometimes, if you can—only a little."[8]

In the final scene Twain makes his intention clear by following the burlesque child-courtship with the beginning of an adult one:

Saturday.—I am happy again, and forever, this time. I've seen her! I've seen the girl that is my doom [Laura Miller, aged nineteen]. I shall die if I cannot get her. The first time I looked at her I fell in love with her. She looked at me twice in church yesterday, and Oh how I felt. She was with her mother and her brother. When they came out of church I followed them, and twice she looked back and smiled, and I would have smiled too, but there was a tall young man by my side and I was afraid he would notice. At last she dropped a leaf of a flower— rose geranium Ma calls it—and I could see by the way she looked that she meant it for me, and when I stooped to pick it up the tall young man stooped too. I got it, but I felt awful sheepish, and I think he did, too, because he blushed. He asked me for it, and I had to give it to him, though I'd rather given him my bleeding heart, but I pinched off just a little piece and kept it, and shall keep it forever.

The implication is that the tall young man will place the geranium leaf next his heart, just as Billy placed Amy's molasses candy next his; from that point presumably the young man's romance will parallel Billy's.

The sketch contains enough evidence to form a tantalizing suggestion that its specific target is David Copperfield's courtship of Dora. Two names in the burlesque point toward Dickens' novels: Bob Sawyer recalls the medical student in *Pickwick Papers* and Amy, the heroine of *Little Dorrit*. Other bits of evidence point toward *David Copperfield*. Billy calls Amy "my little wife" several times just as David habitually refers to Dora as "my little wife" and "dear, dear little wife" after their marriage. Amy lavishes affection upon her dog Bingo in a manner reminiscent of Dora's attachment to Jip. In mentality Amy is quite similar to Dora despite the disparity in physical ages, a fact especially noticeable in Amy's idea of a suitable house for her and Billy, "a little cosy cottage with vines running over the windows and a four-story brick attached where she could receive company and give parties." David dreams of just such a cottage after he learns of his aunt's ruin; the four-story addition is the sort of thing Dora would need for all the entertaining she plans. The geranium leaf for which Billy and the tall young man vie serves to recall the geraniums which figure so prominently in David's courtship. They fill the greenhouse where David passes his first moments alone with Dora and comprise the bouquet he brings to her birthday party. Indeed, he himself confesses the great importance of this particular flower in his courtship:

The scent of a geranium leaf, at this day, strikes me with a half comical, half serious wonder as to what change has come over me in a moment; and then I see a straw hat and blue ribbons, and a quantity of curls, and a little black dog being held up, in two slender arms, against a bank of blossoms and bright leaves.[9]

In addition to such indications, "The Boy's Manuscript" includes in its action certain parallels to David's courtship. Like David, Billy is an avid window-watcher. David circles Dora's house like "a moon-struck slave," stretching his chin above the palings and "blowing kisses at the lights in the windows." Billy, however, is to some extent better rewarded than David, for he sees part of a dress flutter past the appropriate window. But the resultant ecstasy is short-lived: "But by and bye it turned out that that was the nigger chambermaid fluttering her dress at the window, and then I felt so down-hearted I wished I had never found it out." Like David, Billy does an amazing amount of walking in hopes of a chance to be seen by or to see his beloved. David, in his vanity, cripples himself with shoes much too small for his feet, but still he walks. Billy plays hooky in order to walk Amy's street; he joins the torchlight procession and persuades it to pass her house four times. In other respects the two courtships are similar: the frequently broken engagement, the rivalry with Red Whisker, and the flirtation with the lady in pink in an attempt to arouse jealousy in Dora all have parallels in "The Boy's Manuscript."

It is difficult to believe Twain was unaware that these resemblances would suggest *David Copperfield* to his readers, for he knew his Dickens early and well. In 1862, he was not only familiar with but deeply read in at least one novel by Dickens; in a letter to William H. Clagget from Carson City, dated February 28, 1862, he quotes lines from *Dombey and Sons* from memory: "I hope I'm not an oyster though I may not wish to live in crowds." He continues by

naming a number of characters from the book, describing them with
an unmistakable relish, and ends the passage with the remark, "Oh,
d—n it, I wish I had the book."[10] Walter Blair asserts, "There is
much evidence that, from the 1860's on, Twain knew various writings of Dickens quite well."[11] Henry W. Fischer quotes a remark
made by Twain in 1879, "You know I have always been a great
admirer of Dickens, and his 'Tale of Two Cities' I read at least every
two years. Dickens witnessed my first holding hands with Livy when
I took her to one of his lectures in New York.... I have finished 'The
Tale of Two Cities' for the 'steenth time."[12] The Dickens reading the
night Twain first held hands with Livy was the storm scene from
David Copperfield, the death of James Steerforth.[13]

As suggestive as such evidence is, it is not conclusive. Indeed,
although the burlesque in many respects parallels David's romance,
it also includes aspects of the nineteenth-century literary courtship which do not appear in *David Copperfield,* an indication that
although Dickens' novel may have been the special target, Mark
Twain scattered his shot more widely. An impoverished lover in
more senses than the financial one, David has no memento from
Dora to wear next his heart. Billy surpasses him in this respect, even
if the memento is a piece of molasses candy. "I put it next my heart,
and it got warm and stuck, and it won't come off, and I can't get my
shirt off, but I don't mind it." David claims to worship the very
ground upon which Dora walks, but he is more inhibited in his
devotions than Billy. After leaving his suicide note at Amy's door,
Billy writes, "Then I looked up at her window a long time, and
prayed that she might be forgiven for what I was going to do—
and then cried and kissed the ground where she used to step out at
the door, and took a pinch of the dirt and put it next my heart where
the candy was." David fails to languish under the fever of his ill-
concealed love; he becomes footsore and weary from his walking,
but he does not sicken, take to his bed, and hover near death. In
this phase of the nineteenth-century literary courtship, he is outdone
by Thackeray's Arthur Pendennis, who almost dies as a result of his

infatuation for Fanny Bolton. In suffering, Billy is more like Pendennis, even if his prostration does result from his mother's vigorous application of various home remedies in her effort to cure him of his love-induced lethargy.

Mark Twain achieves a part of his burlesque effect by reducing the principals in the courtship to children of about the age of eight. The device is an old one in burlesque, apparently first used by Fielding in his *Tragedy of Tragedies; or The Life and Death of Tom Thumb, the Great* (1730). Twain, however, did not dip so far back in the history of burlesque for his model; instead, he drew his idea from a burlesque troupe he had seen in Carson City. When he refers to *Jack the Giant Killer* in Billy's account of his theatrical endeavors with Wart Hopkins, he is referring to an extravaganza in the repertory of R. G. Marsh's Juvenile Comedians, a burlesque troupe composed of boys and girls ranging in age from six to sixteen years. Twain saw this troupe during its stay in Carson City in January, 1864, and recorded his impressions of it in his letter to the *Enterprise* dated January 13, 1864. In his letter, Twain mentions only *Toodles, The Limerick Boy,* and *Barney the Baron,* but undoubtedly the performances at Carson included *Jack the Giant Killer* as well.[14]

Ordinarily writers using this burlesque device rely upon the incongruity between the actions of the principals and their age and physical size, somewhat in the same manner as Swift relied upon the disparity between action and size in his Lilliputians, but Twain has introduced an innovation; retaining the general course of the adult romance, he translates its love-letters, mementos, events, and characters into the notes, gifts, accidents, and people supposedly typical of his own boyhood in Hannibal. Thus the love-letters become ungrammatical and misspelled notes on copybook papers, the cherished flower becomes a chunk of molasses candy, the jealousies become fist fights with other schoolboys, and the characters in part—although it would be difficult to say to what extent—are portraits of Twain's Hannibal schoolmates. The humor of the burlesque depends to a great measure upon the refusal of other characters in the fictive world to recognize and sympathize with the lover's trials. Billy's mother, for example, fails to identify his symptoms as those of love-sickness and treats Billy for such childhood illnesses as measles and bile and finally in frustration heaps upon him a whole series of treatments, trying to cure him "in a sort of a *general* way." Surely love was never tried so sorely.

Because the burlesque is, as DeVoto says, the first use Twain has made of the Hannibal material, "it has a far from slight importance in the history of American literature and even of world literature."[15] But it has another and, for the purposes of this discussion, a greater importance: it is an epitome of the plot which furnishes the structure of *Tom Sawyer.* In the work as finally published, the names of the principals have been changed; Amy Johnson has become Becky Thatcher and Billy Rogers is transformed into Tom Sawyer. Numerous episodes and two subplots have been added, but underneath these changes and additions runs the same thread, a burlesque courtship, the events of which serve to hold the whole work together. Acting upon the evidence afforded by the opening chapter, Walter Blair attributes the structure of the novel to the contemporary literature about the model boy. He traces this theme and concludes that *Tom Sawyer* is "a fictional working-out of the author's antipathy to the conventional plot structure of juvenile tales."[16] Certainly burlesque of model-boy literature is a prominent element in *Tom Sawyer;* as Blair points out, the first chapter of the book is devoted to displaying in Tom characteristics which label him clearly as a Bad Boy. Furthermore, Twain makes the point explicit when he writes, "He was not the Model Boy of the village. He knew the model boy very well though—and loathed him." But to conclude that the basic structure of the book comes from model-boy literature is inaccurate. The theme of model boy versus bad boy, concentrated in the first five chapters, occupies a relatively small amount of space in the novel. It dominates Chapters I, IV, and V and makes a brief appearance in the opening of Chapter III. But from Chapter VI to the end of the book it disappears; more important evidence that it is a subordinate theme appears, however, in Chapter IV, where, it will be recalled, Tom surprises everyone by coming forward with sufficient tickets to claim the prize Bible. His method of collecting tickets is another facet of the model-boy burlesque, but his purpose in claiming the prize has to do with the burlesque courtship: he does it to gain prestige in the eyes of the beautiful, blue-eyed creature who has captured his heart. By claiming the prize, he not only will focus her attention on him but will also be able to take a place on the platform with her and her family. The model-boy theme thus becomes contributory to the central plot, Tom's courtship of Becky.

Similarly the other major episodes in the novel are subordinate and contributory to the courtship theme. Twice the uneven course of his wooing leads Tom to forsake home and country for a life of forlorn wandering. In the first instance, occasioned by Becky's reaction to his inadvertent mention of Amy Lawrence, he, like Werther, contemplates suicide. But, unable to die "temporarily," he resolves instead to run away, to become a pirate, to return one day as "Tom Sawyer the Pirate!—the Black Avenger of the Spanish Main!" Interrupted in his flight by Joe Harper, he forgets his bloody purpose in the thrill of playing Robin Hood. The second instance is more fruitful because it leads to the famous Jackson's Island episode. This second withdrawal results when Becky refuses to respond to Tom's attempted reconciliation. Once again, Tom determines, in his sorrow, to become a pirate. Out of his resolve grows the piratical partnership of Tom Sawyer, the Black Avenger of the Spanish Main; Huck Finn, the Red-Handed; and Joe Harper, the Terror of the Seas. The retreat to Jackson's Island, actually the temporary death for which Tom sighs during the first withdrawal, has the appropriate effect upon Becky, although a reconciliation does not result because of Tom's desire to give her a taste of the same medicine she had given him.

Even the knowledge of real murder, the threat of real vengeance, and the hope of real treasure cannot outweigh the courtship in Tom's mind. The climactic event of a night begun with Injun Joe's murder of Dr. Robinson and ended with Bull Harbison's ominous

howling over Muff Potter is Becky's return of the engagement gift.
Tom is even able to forget the moral dilemma provoked by Injun
Joe's betrayal of Muff Potter. "One of the reasons why Tom's mind
had drifted away from its secret troubles was, that it had found a
new and weighty matter to interest itself about. Becky Thatcher had
stopped coming to school." The discovery that she is ill and the
thought that she might die crowd all else from his mind. He main-
tains his lonely vigil, yearning and languishing, and as in "The
Boy's Manuscript" the result is a vigorous application of home-reme-
dies by his aunt, an application culminating in the Pain-Killer episode. Clearly, as far as Tom is concerned, nothing is more important
than Becky.

Structurally, the courtship thread is inextricably tangled with
the Injun Joe thread. The meeting with Huck Finn leading to the
midnight rendezvous and the witnessing of the murder also serves
Tom in wooing Becky, for only after he notices the vacant seat beside
her does he explain his tardiness to the schoolmaster by loudly pro-
claiming he had stopped to talk with Huck. When Tom and Huck
dig for treasure on the hill beyond Still-House branch, Tom explains
that if he finds treasure, he is "going to buy a new drum, and a sure-
'nough sword, and a red necktie and a bull pup, and get married."
Obviously the bride-to-be is Becky. During the search for a treasure
which is to finance Tom's marriage, the two learn of an actual
treasure when they spy on Injun Joe. The picnic, resulting both in
the final reconciliation of the lovers and in the discovery of Injun
Joe's treasure, has its origin in Becky's desire to spite Tom. In the
common end of the two threads, however, the ascendancy of the
courtship plot clearly appears, for they both culminate in Judge
Thatcher's blessings upon his daughter's lover, the traditional conclusion to all such courtships.

The process followed by Mark Twain in expanding the original
short burlesque, "The Boy's Manuscript," into a novel now becomes
clear. He has added two subplots, one of which, the Tom-Sid rivalry,
is basically, as Blair has pointed out, a burlesque of the model-boy

literature. In addition, he has inserted several episodes, most of which
bear rather closely upon the major plot or one of the subplots:
whitewashing the fence, the church service and pinch-bug sequence,
the Robin Hood game with Joe Harper, the Jackson's Island
sequence, and examination day at the school. All except the whitewashing scene either include or verge upon actual burlesque.
Although not literary burlesque, the church-service episode is certainly a burlesque of a typical small-town Sunday service, and examination day at the school furnishes an opportunity to burlesque
oratory, compositions, and recitations. The two withdrawals, the
Robin Hood episode with Joe Harper and the Jackson's Island episode, are not burlesque of the literature upon which they are based,
for the reader's attention is drawn not so much to the literature
behind the episodes as to the actions of the three boys. But even so,
Mark Twain shows a dependence upon the background literature
quite similar in its parasitism to the dependence of the writer of
burlesque upon his targets, and one cannot say that Robin Hood
and Ned Buntline, whose *Black Avenger of the Spanish Main* and
kindred romances figure so prominently in life on Jackson's Island,
escape unscathed from Tom, Joe, and Huck. In short, Mark Twain's
method of composition in *Tom Sawyer* is quite analogous to his
method in "Mamie Grant" and the travel narratives. He has used
the plot of "The Boy's Manuscript" for his "running narrative-
plank" and inserted episodes and subplots, a number of which are
burlesques or near-burlesques, to make his novel. Structurally the
result is quite like *Roughing It* in that the inserted material is neatly
fitted into place and connected to the frame plot.

Aside from his bad-boy traits, Tom's chief characteristic is one
inherited from Mamie Grant and the tenderfoot traveler in *Roughing It:* the tendency to live life "by the book," to see things through
"the mellow moonshine of romance." Structurally, his function is
the same as Mamie's and the tenderfoot's. By characterizing him
thus, Twain is able to include within the frame of his story a number
of references to other books. However, in *Tom Sawyer* the device

does not result in the irony of "Mamie Grant" nor does it produce a theme of disillusionment comparable to that of *Roughing It*. Although Tom's head is filled with the plots of numerous romances, he does not confuse his daydreams with reality. He has no need to do so: one of the most remarkable facts about the fictive world of *Tom Sawyer* is that the reality with its Injun Joe and buried treasure corresponds closely to Tom's romance-inspired notions. In such a world disillusionment is impossible.

As an authority on the authorities, Tom assumes a relationship with his companions resembling quite closely the Mr. Twain–Mr. Brown character-axis of the travel narratives. Tutor in the proper forms of engagement, Tom does not let Becky rest until she has conformed to the ritual required by his authorities, vague as the identity of those authorities may be. Joe Harper recognizes Tom's scholarship to the extent that he dies as Guy of Guisborne should without a murmur of protest. But neither Joe nor Becky has much resemblance to Brown, even if they are less knowledgeable in the "authorities." Neither of them is a "bitter enemy to sentiment," and Joe's protest when he finds the book will not permit him to kill Robin Hood is the nearest either comes to revolt. He exclaims, "Well, it's blamed mean,—that's all." But the revolt goes no further: "there was no getting around the authorities."

In the relationship between Tom and Huck, however, both ends of the character-axis are fully developed. Despite his bad-boy traits, Tom is definitely among the respectable boys in comparison to Huck. "Tom was like the rest of the respectable boys, in that he envied Huckleberry his gaudy outcast condition, and was under strict orders not to play with him." In St. Petersburg, "respectability" is composed of many things, but among the children who figure in the action of the novel one of its outstanding components is the acceptance of Tom's position as interpreter of the "authorities." Unlike the other children, Huck, untouched by literary influences, is relatively unimpressed by Tom's learning. In the retreat to Jackson's Island, Joe Harper joins Tom in the imaginative reconstruction of observed reality and concedes "that there were some conspicuous advantages about a life of crime, and so he consented to be a pirate." Huck joins Tom and Joe in piracy, but he has none of the book-inspired enthusiasm of the others. "He joined them promptly, for all careers were one to him; he was indifferent." On the island, Tom and Joe draw their pleasure from the belief that they are actually experiencing the life of pirates. Huck concedes that life on Jackson's Island is "gay" and is "the *nuts*" but for a much different reason: "I don't want nothing better'n this. I don't ever get enough to eat, gen'ally—and here they can't come and pick at a feller and bullyrag him so." Because he sees some personal advantage in what they are doing, he is willing to submit to being "the Red-Handed." But the authorities must meet the test of his inclination and experience or be discarded. When Tom tells him that as a hermit he has "got to sleep on the hardest place he can find, and put sackcloth and ashes on his head, and stand out in the rain," his reply is, "Dern'd if I would," and Tom's insistence that he would "*have* to" fails to shake him. Totally unimpressed by the prerogatives of kingship, he sees only the fact that kings, like the Negro slaves in St. Petersburg, have only one name. "Well, if they like it, Tom, all right; but I don't want to be a king and have only just a given name, like a nigger." Tom's determination to marry moves him to comment, "Well, that's the foolishest thing you could do. Look at Pap and my mother. Fight! Why, they used to fight all the time. I remember, mighty well." In his view of observed reality he is, obviously, the same as the Mr. Brown who insisted on including the " 'santipedes,' and cockroaches, and fleas, and lizards, and red ants, and scorpions, and spiders, and mosquitoes and missionaries" in Mr. Twain's idyllic description of Honolulu.

Although within the character-axis Huck is as far along the scale of unregeneracy as Mr. Brown, Tom is, despite his bookishness, not quite so far along the scale of refinement as Mr. Twain, partly because of his bad-boy traits, partly because of his language, almost as uncultivated as Huck's, and partly because of his propensity, originally that of the "Oracle" in *The Innocents Abroad,* to misinterpret his authorities. In seeing that Joe Harper plays Robin Hood the way it should be played, Tom explains, "The book says, 'Then with one back-handed stroke he slew poor Guy of Guisborne.' You're to turn around and let me hit you in the back."

In the construction of *Tom Sawyer,* then, in plot, characterization, and character relations, Twain has drawn heavily upon the tools and skills he had developed in his burlesques and travel narratives; simultaneously, he has drawn, as in "The Boy's Manuscript," upon his own boyhood in Hannibal. The resultant novel makes a curiously mixed impression upon the reader. In the courtship plot, Tom is much too mature for his age, a circumstance only to be expected since the frame plot grew from a burlesque in which the principal device is the attributing of adult actions to a child. In those portions of Tom's character and adventures derived from Twain's memories of his own childhood, Tom and his life are Twain's idealization of boyhood at about the age of eight or nine. In the conflict between burlesque and nostalgia, one can discern what Twain had in mind when he wavered between making *Tom Sawyer* a book for adults or one for children. On July 5, 1875, he wrote to Howells that *Tom Sawyer* was a book for adults, but seven months later he wrote that the book was to be one for children. In the second letter he indicates what alterations were necessary to meet the new purpose: "I finally concluded to cut the Sunday school speech down to the first two sentences, leaving no suggestion of satire, since the book is to be for boys and girls."[17] Although Twain uses the word *satire,* a reflection of his original purpose, the speech in question is in technique a parody, as the remaining fragment shows, closely connected with the burlesque of Sunday-school literature which forms one of the major themes of the book. In studying the revisions in the manuscript, DeVoto found further reductions in the amount of burlesque.[18] For the obvious reason that burlesque presupposes the reader's ability to perceive in the exaggerations and distortions of the burlesque the distinctive qualities in style, plot, or characterization of the target work, Twain had to reduce the amount of burlesque in *Tom Sawyer* when, by changing the desired audience to boys and girls, he could no longer depend upon his reader's astuteness. In the revision he could not eliminate all the burlesque because the frame plot itself is a burlesque; consequently the conflict between burlesque and nostalgia remains a characteristic of the book and results in what DeVoto calls its gravest limitation: "... that the boys are of no particular age and therefore much that they do and feel is psychological anachronism." As burlesque figures representing the principals of an adult courtship, Tom and Becky must act older than they are; when their courtship becomes the frame for a boyhood idyl, psychological anachronism must result. But as DeVoto says, "It is silly to ask how old Tom and Huck are."[19] The world in which Tom, Huck, Joe, and Becky live is not a world governed by a literal application of the laws of probability: hidden as it is among the other improbabilities, the Tom-Becky courtship strikes no discordant note. The book is not only one of Twain's most carefully constructed novels; it is also what Twain called it, "a hymn, put into prose form to give it a worldly air."[20]

II

Thus in genesis and structure *Tom Sawyer* is in many respects quite comparable to *Joseph Andrews*, although the burlesque frame is much more clearly visible in Fielding's novel. Like *The Innocents Abroad* it is a transition piece, a link between total burlesque and total originality. In his next novel, *The Prince and the Pauper*, Twain completely freed himself of the burlesque attitude and intent, although he still relied upon devices developed in burlesque for the solution of structural problems. When he undertook the composition of this "grave and stately" book, his writer's tool chest was not yet fully stocked, and he himself was still an apprentice in the craft of the novel. A modification of the structural solution of *Tom Sawyer*, an early burlesque appropriated for a frame, served to give direction to the events in *The Prince and the Pauper*, but such a solution did not supply another lack: the absence of purpose, theme, or moral.

The basic structure of the book is summarized in Twain's note-book entry for November 23, 1877: "Edward VI and a little pauper exchange places by accident a day or so before Henry VIII's death. The prince wanders in rags and hardships and the pauper suffers the (to him) horrible miseries of princedom, up to the moment of crowning in Westminster Abbey, when proof is brought and the mistake rectified."[21] Upon the central twisted strand of exchanged identities, the Miles Hendon subplot and the various episodes are strung. The main plot is simple and symmetrical in its outline. As Edward sinks from luxury to poverty and hardship and rises once again to his former luxury, Tom Canty rises from poverty to luxury and sinks again, although not to such a depth as that from which he started. Into Edward's adventures Twain has woven the Miles Hendon subplot and the various episodes illustrative of Edward's education concerning his own laws, and into Tom's, his difficulties in the role of prince and successor to the throne.[22]

The source of this structure, by common agreement among critics the most symmetrical Twain ever devised, is the "Burlesque L'Homme Qui Rit," apparently prepared for the Buffalo Express but never published. Paine dates the manuscript 1869 or 1870, but 1869 seems the more likely date. At the end of the burlesque, Twain wrote, "I have sandwiched in some thirty or forty lines of the Apple-ton's translation of Victor Hugo's 'L'Homme Qui Rit,' "[23] a trans-lation by William Young published in 1869 by D. Appleton and Company. Essentially a failure as a burlesque, the piece is neverthe-less the most important of Twain's experiments with the burlesque novel during his Bohemian apprenticeship, for, like the "Legend of the Spectacular Ruin" in A Tramp Abroad, it is a hybrid resulting from the attempt to combine a burlesque of a literary work and the serious allegorical treatment of an original theme.

It starts as an excellent burlesque of Hugo's novel and a quite competent parody of his style, or, more properly, of his style as reflected in Young's translation. Chapter I closely parallels the novel, recounting Gwynplaine's abandonment by the Comprachicos and his wanderings upon the Portland Bill. Burlesque gives way, however, to allegory when Gwynplaine encounters the body swinging from the gibbet: "Suspended to [the gallows] was a shapeless mass. A shapeless mass, hung in chains. A putrid carcass—, with obscene ravens flapping their heavy wings about the eyeless face. A horrible, ghastly, decaying party, this boy saw—a party labeled 'AFRICAN SLAVE TRADE,' on the mutiliated seat of his trowsers." From this point, although he follows the events of *L'Homme qui rit,* Twain writes open allegory. Chapter II, entitled "The Ark," opens with the statement, "The Ark 'African Slavery' (otherwise the ark) was out in the storm that awful night." Like the Biscay hooker, the ark springs a leak and begins to founder:

Overboard with the freight! Overboard with the express packages! Overboard with the mails!
A pause.
Overboard with the baggage!

In small letters above the word *baggage,* Twain has written "means slaves."

The Stranger, whom Twain labels "Confederacy," then prepares a document revealing Gwynplaine's birth, seals it in a bottle, and throws it overboard just as the ark sinks. Meanwhile Gwynplaine and his beloved Dea, identified in the allegory as Democracy, have joined an itinerant troupe of actors. At Southwark, Gwynplaine is thrown into jail, but when the brandy bottle comes ashore, he is released and made an earl. He seeks "vengeance upon the class that had once abused him—that had now lifted him to the clouds. At last he compassed it."

He went before the greatest tribunal in the land—before the mighty People.
He made a speech....
He told how he had played all the characters known to the profession —Alderman, Mayor, Legislator, Congressman, Senator, Vice President,

President! He told them what they were coming to, & left the Constitution with them. Also the flag, with thirty-six stars on it.
That speech finished *him.*

With only a few exceptions toward the end of the piece, Twain has followed the plot of *L'Homme qui rit* quite faithfully, trying to impose upon it, through allegory, a theme and a message which were, evidently, important to him. The result, however, is imperfect. The theme in Chapters I and II seems to be clear: slavery and the Confederacy are the targets of Twain's attack, but the allegory becomes confused after the revelation of Gwynplaine's identity. As in the original novel, he is by birth a member of the aristocracy. In the allegory, then, is he supposed to be affiliated with the Confederacy? In light of the situation in the target novel, such an interpretation seems invalid, for Gwynplaine is an aristocrat betrayed by the aristocracy, and upon this class, the class "that had once abused him," he seeks vengeance. In the allegory, the aristocracy, distinct from the group on the ark headed by the Stranger labeled "Confederacy," has no allegorical significance. Further problems of interpretation center on Gwynplaine, who seems to have no clearly perceivable symbolic function in the allegory. Twain suppresses the facial deformity which proved Gwynplaine's downfall in the novel and instead attributes his failure to the fickleness of the people to whom he appeals in his speech. In two brief sentences, Gwynplaine shifts from an actor playing "all the characters known to the profession," that is, all the political roles from alderman to President, to an actual lawgiver who leaves the Constitution and the flag with the people he is addressing.

After his initial failure, Twain abandoned allegory and instead used the structure of the burlesque for the frame of *The Prince and the Pauper.* Because his purpose in the revision and expansion of his burlesque was no longer that of ridiculing Hugo but was now almost the same as Hugo's, it becomes exceedingly difficult to distinguish between the burlesque and its target when one tries to identify the immediate source of Twain's structural pattern.

Generally, in attitude, tone, and treatment, the two books are almost identical. In *The Prince and the Pauper,* Twain illustrates both in Edward VI and in Tom Canty how poverty fosters mercy and justice. After becoming a victim of his own laws and after seeing the sufferings of others under them, the young king concludes that "the world is made wrong, kings should go to school to their own laws at times, and so learn mercy." Similarly, Hugo's Gwynplaine, after his experiences as an itinerant actor, hopes to reform the laws by informing the lords of what he has suffered:

What advantage to be, in the midst of [the House of Lords], the one man who has seen, touched, undergone, suffered; and to be able to exclaim to them:—"I have been close to that wherefrom you are far off"—to those aristocrats yet full of illusions. He will throw the reality into their faces; and they will tremble, for it will be true; and they will applaud, for it will be grand.[24]

The two parts of Gwynplaine's life, first as poverty-stricken actor, then as nobleman, suggest the adventures of both Prince Edward and Tom Canty. Son of Baron Clancharlie, Gwynplaine is sold by order of the king to the Comprachicos, who mutilate him in such a manner as to make his face a comic mask. Abandoned when the Comprachicos flee England after the accession of William and Mary, he joins Ursus and lives as an itinerant actor. While the troupe is in Southwark, he learns of his heritage and is suddenly elevated to his rightful place as Baron Clancharlie. After an over-elaborate investiture with the robes and other appurtenances of his office, he enters the House of Lords intending to lead the peers in the reforms his own experiences have shown are much needed. The Lords, however, are amused by his pretentions and laugh him down. In despair he gives up his title and returns to his former friends, who have been ordered to leave the country. When Dea dies on the ship, Gwyplaine commits suicide.

Hugo does not detail the earlier portions of Gwynplaine's life, his sale to the Comprachicos and his life among them. The book begins with Gwynplaine's abandonment at Portland, the necessary facts about his prior life being given later. Taking such hints as Hugo furnishes, Twain has built from the first portion of Gwynplaine's life a consecutive narrative with Prince Edward as hero. The beggar band with which Edward is forced to travel from Southwark into the Kentish countryside is quite comparable to the band of Comprachicos, with, however, a slight difference: the Comprachicos, according to Hugo, dealt only in the mutilation of children whom they had gained by legal methods and in all else refrained from crime. The beggar band is far outside the law. But Hugo is not quite consistent on the point, for in describing the various punishments meted out to members of the Comprachico gang he mentions burnings for witchcraft, brandings for thievery and beggary, and mutilations for various crimes. Indeed, the first few chapters of Hugo's book, emphasizing the inhuman practices both of the Comprachicos and of the law and given an air of authenticity by the citation of authorities, resemble very much in tone and subject the central chapters of Twain's novel.

Although Twain has adhered to the general outlines of Gwynplaine's early history in the story of Prince Edward, he has borrowed from the latter portion the scene in which Gwynplaine is ridiculed by his fellow lords. Gwynplaine's humiliation is precipitated by his grotesque mutilation, the eternal grin cut into his face by the renowned surgeon of the Comprachicos. His inability to control his facial expression provokes a spontaneous outburst of laughter, but the laughter continues and insults follow because the lords refuse to recognize him as Lord Clancharlie and persist in seeing only Gwynplaine, the vagrant actor. Like Gwynplaine, Edward is ridiculed in the midst of an earnest endeavor to right a wrong, but Edward's humiliation comes at the hands of beggars, not of Lords. As in the case of Gwynplaine, however, Edward's humiliation results from his audience's refusal to ignore his apparent background. The beggars see only a lad in rags pretending to be King

Edward VI and treat him accordingly, crowning him "Foo-foo the First, king of the Mooncalves."

For both Gwynplaine and Edward, the result of the experiences among the poverty-stricken is the same. They learn to be merciful. When they return to their rightful places among the nobility, their messages to the other nobles are the same. In his speech before the House of Lords, Gwynplaine says, "Oh! have pity! Oh! you know not this fatal world, whereto you believe that you belong. So high, you are outside of it. I will tell you what it is. I have had experience. I come up from beneath pressure. I can tell you how much you weigh."[25] King Edward, "when some great dignitary, some gilded vassal of the crown, made argument against his leniency," replies in much the same fashion, "'What dost *thou* know of suffering and oppression? I and my people know, but not thou.'"

With the exception of the humiliation scene in the House of Lords, Gwynplaine's experiences after he is restored to his title furnish the outline for Tom Canty's experiences at the palace. Completely bewildered by his sudden elevation, Gwynplaine is totally unprepared to cope with the various rituals. He is guided, therefore, by the Usher of the Black Rod and the Garter King-At-Arms, who whisper instructions to him as he faces each crisis in the ceremonials. Tom, similarly bewildered, also has two helpful guides, Hertford and St. John. In the matter of the ceremonies themselves, the attitudes of Hugo and Twain are quite comparable. Hugo's description of Gwynplaine's investiture at the House of Lords with its ritualistic presentation of the three kings-at-arms, six dukes-at-arms, and the four pursuivants-at-arms verges on comedy, so much so that Hugo has felt the necessity of saying, "It is probable that the House of Lords will not recognize itself in what you have just read and in what you are going to read, any more than a pretty woman of other days, who desires not to have wrinkles."[26] That Hugo intended to be humorous in these passages is doubtful, but Twain draws excellent and unmistakable comedy from the palace ceremonials.

Prior to his experiences at the palace as pseudo-prince, Tom Canty is quite an unusual beggar-boy. He seems conscious of a latent nobility within him which prevents him from accepting his lot and finally drives him to create a royal court, to cast himself in the role of prince, and to surround himself with a mock nobility. In this characteristic he is like Gwynplaine, who, although he did not go so far as to act out his latent nobility, nevertheless felt his superiority to those around him:

—Ah! cried he—for there are cries from the depths of thought—ah! it was thus, then, I was a lord. All is revealed.... Well might I feel something else than a miserable wretch palpitating underneath my rags; and when I turned to the side of men, well might I feel that they were the flock, and that I was—not the dog, but—the shepherd. Pastors of peoples, leaders of men, guides and masters—that is what my forefathers were; and what they were, I am![27]

The major difference between the two books is the fact that in *The Prince and the Pauper* Gwynplaine's story is divided between two characters, Prince Edward and Tom Canty. Hugo, himself, however, makes just such a division, splitting Gwynplaine into two personalities, thus furnishing the hint for the actual division: "Gwynplaine had in his brain ... the shock of the past against the future, two Gwynplaines, himself doubled—in the background, a child in rags, emerging from darkness, prowling round, shivering, hungered, causing laughter—in the foreground, a brilliant nobleman, ostentatious, superb, dazzling London."[28] The division in Gwynplaine becomes not merely one of past and future but one involving two conflicting halves of a single being, "two phantoms, adversity and prosperity, taking possession of the same soul and pulling it each a different way. Sad partition of an intelligence, a will, a brain, between these two hostile brothers, the poor spectre and the rich spectre. Abel and Cain in the same man."[29] Because the ultimate source of *The Prince and the Pauper* is Hugo's *L'Homme qui rit,* it is only fitting that while Prince Edward is with the gang of beggars his chief tormentor is a rogue named Hugo. But differences in emphasis and theme indicate that the immediate source was not Hugo's novel, but Twain's burlesque of it. Both Twain and Hugo attack the aristocrat's insensibility to the sufferings of the people beneath him, but the direction of the attack is different in the two novels. Hugo dwells not upon the plight of the common people but upon the life of the aristocracy, exposing through such characters as David Dirry-Moir and the various peers in the House of Lords the aristocrat's total lack of humane consideration for others. Twain takes the opposite direction; he denounces the aristocrat's insensibility by concentrating upon the oppression of the common people. He is thus able to work into his novel the attack on slavery which in his burlesque he had tried to present through allegory. The difference in emphasis is reflected in the contrast between the two humiliation episodes. To achieve his purpose, Hugo introduces among the peers one who has learned to think and feel as the common people do. The lords, insensible to the demands of mercy, laugh when Gwynplaine denounces the expenditure of money for aristocratic luxuries. In *The Prince and the Pauper* the situation is reversed as it is in the burlesque. Like the burlesque Gwynplaine, Edward is the lawgiver among the people; he is before "the greatest tribunal in the land." The humiliation, as in the burlesque, results from a declaration on the question of slavery. Yokel, the farmer, finishes the history of his persecution with the announcement that he is now a slave and, if caught, must hang. Edward overhears him and declares, "Thou shalt *not!*—and this day the end of that law is come!" As in the burlesque, "that speech finished *him*."

Only one sequence in *The Prince and the Pauper* seems to have come directly from Hugo's novel without first filtering through the burlesque: the series of episodes detailing Tom Canty's difficulties with palace ceremonials. These episodes parallel rather closely Gwynplaine's investiture as a peer in the House of Lords and consequently, since this section is omitted in the burlesque, must be derived directly from the novel. With this one exception, Twain's book owes its structural pattern to the early "Burlesque *L'Homme Qui Rit.*"

Within the framework thus gleaned from his burlesque, Twain has followed a structural pattern quite similar to that of *Tom Sawyer* and the travel narratives. That is, the general plot-outline is used merely as a narrative-plank along which the author has arranged the various episodes and the one subplot of the novel. In the first three chapters, he disposes of preliminary matters and accomplishes the exchange. The next nine chapters, Chapters IV to XII, form a unit in which Twain has attempted to counterpoise the episodes devoted to Tom and Edward. Tom Canty's interview with King Henry is balanced by Edward's meeting with John Canty. Similarly, as Tom is aided through his difficulties at court by Hertford and St. John, so is Edward guided by Miles Hendon. And finally Tom's first royal dinner has its counterpart in Edward's dinner with Miles.

But Twain does not sustain the balance; episodes, more or less humorous in tone, devoted to Tom's experiences with court ceremonials predominate in the first half of the book. In Chapter XV, a distinct change in attitude toward Tom as prince occurs, for at this point Twain ceases to exploit the humor of Tom's situation and turns instead to the task of exposing the cruelty of the laws and of illustrating the quality of mercy which poverty and hardship foster. The change is the more evident because Chapter XV, in which Tom tries and acquits the accused witch and the condemned murderer, follows immediately after the most humorous chapter in the book, Twain's description of the dressing ceremony. Furthermore, Chapter XIV contains an instance of "justice" which is a sharp contrast to the justice exemplified in Chapter XV. The interview with the whipping-boy reaches its climax when Tom makes him Hereditary Grand Whipping-Boy and promises, "I will betake me to my books again, and study so ill that they must in justice treble thy wage, so mightily shall the business of thine office be augmented." The concept of justice here is certainly quite different from that which guides Tom in the next chapter during the interview with the witch and the murderer. The new attitude governs the remainder of the episodes in which Tom figures. The change in attitude coincides with the beginning of Edward's journey into Kent; that is, with the beginning of the "serious and instructive" portion of the book. The state dinner in Chapter XVI is the last episode concerned with Tom until Chapter XXX, Tom's royal progress on the way to the coronation. The intervening chapters, XVII to XXIX, deal with Edward's adventures in Kent and his education.

The change in plan and attitude visible in Chapters XVI and XVII indicates the point where, as Twain says, a hiatus occurred in the writing of the novel. Years later he recalled that he ran into difficulties at this point and laid the manuscript aside for two years. In a recollection dictated in 1906, he says,

When I have been writing a book I have pigeonholed it without misgivings when its tank ran dry, well knowing that it would fill up within the next two or three years, and that then the work of completing it would be simple and easy. *The Prince and the Pauper* struck work in the middle...and I did not touch it again for two years.[30]

The cause of the stoppage was, apparently, structural, for when Twain returned to the novel he abandoned the attempt to balance Tom's and Edward's experiences and to exploit the comedy of Tom's situation. Structurally Tom as prince offers no great problem. Once he is installed in the palace, Twain could go on almost indefinitely extracting comedy from his reactions to the various court rituals. But with Prince Edward as beggar the problem is somewhat different. If Edward was to serve the instructive purpose designed for him, Twain needed some modification of his frame. By borrowing his frame plot from the early burlesque as he did in *Tom Sawyer,* he could organize his fictive world insofar as the order of events was concerned; but, unless his purpose were the same as Hugo's he had to find some device which would permit the addition of his own theme to the novel. To furnish the device, Twain decided to take Edward on a journey and subject him to a series of instructive adventures.

The journey into Kent marks an important new advance in Twain's structural technique, an advance which draws upon his experience in the travel narratives and looks forward to *Huckleberry Finn*. Prince Edward's journey, beginning and ending symmetrically with a separation on London Bridge, is quite comparable to the tenderfoot's journey across the plains in *Roughing It* because each episode contributes to the prince's disillusionment. Before the journey began Edward had, like the tenderfoot, a highly romantic conception of a life of poverty. In his interview with Tom in the palace, he listens eagerly to Tom's description of his life and finally exclaims, "Oh, prithee, say no more, 'tis glorious! If that I could but clothe me in raiment like to thine, and strip my feet, and revel in the mud once, just once, with none to rebuke me or forbid, meseemeth I could forego the crown!" He gets his wish: he foregoes the crown and clothed in rags and poorly shod he "revels" in the mud, but he finds to his sorrow that the reality is quite different from the prevision. He learns that rags give poor protection from the cold and that mud makes a poor couch; he is glad to sleep in straw with a calf for bedfellow.

The journey is the frame for the series of disillusioning episodes, most of them concentrated in the first part of the trip, and for the Miles Hendon subplot. By the time Twain is ready to begin the subplot, he has drifted perilously close to actual burlesque. Just how close appears in the fact that the last episode, the escape from the constable, culminates with a typical burlesque device, the device Twain learned from Webb. When Hendon explains the crime which the constable has committed, he says,

"Yes, it hath a name. In the law this crime is called *Non compos mentis lex talionis sic transit gloria Mundi....* By advantage taken of one in fault, in dire peril, and at thy mercy, thou hast seized goods worth above thirteen pence ha'penny, paying but a trifle for the same; and this, in

the eye of the law, is constructive barratry, misprision of treason, mal-
feasance in office, *ad hominem expurgatis in statu quo*—and the penalty
is death by the halter, without ransom, commutation, or benefit
of clergy."

But Edward's journey differs in one important respect from the
tenderfoot's journey in *Roughing It*. In *The Prince and the Pauper*
the journey is at once a revelation of reality and an education in
moral truth. Thus the journey becomes what may be called a "moral
pilgrimage," for the moral consequences of Edward's disillusionment
are the important matter of the book. As soon as he learns that "the
world is made wrong, kings should go to school to their own laws
at times, and so learn mercy," as soon as he realizes from Hendon's
sacrifice that nobility is a matter of soul, not title, the journey ends
and Twain restores him to the throne. Schematically London Bridge
marks the beginning and end both of the journey and of Edward's
education. When he crosses the bridge from London to Southwark,
he is an arrogant aristocrat; when he crosses it again, from Southwark to London, he is a merciful monarch.[31]

As might be expected, Twain draws upon his past experience in
portraying his two principal characters, Tom Canty and Prince
Edward. Tom Canty, in this respect the more interesting of the two,
combines within himself characteristics typical of both Tom and
Huck in *Tom Sawyer*. Like Tom Sawyer young Canty attempts to
force reality into a pattern formed from his reading in romance. But
Tom Sawyer, although he insists upon doing things "by the book,"
never loses sight, in *Tom Sawyer* at least, of actuality. Tom Canty
does; living "by the book" becomes his normal mode of life: "By
and by Tom's reading and dreaming about princely life wrought
such a strong effect upon him that he began to *act* the prince,
unconsciously."

In his relationship with the prince, however, his role is similar
to that of Huck Finn. To the prince, Tom's enviable lot is to wear
clothes about which no one need feel any concern, to go barefoot,
to fight and swim, and to play in the mud. Edward's envy of Tom

Canty is, in short, the same as that of the "respectable" boys of St.
Petersburg for Huck Finn. From this point until the change in attitude in Chapter XV, Tom Canty is, in conception, a second Huck.
He suddenly and somewhat strangely forgets all he has learned about
court ceremonials from his reading and his practice in the mock
court and has difficulty with even the most common matters of court
etiquette. For example, he must have known from his reading one
of the most rudimentary principles of court ceremony, that no one
sits in the presence of royalty; his own observance in the mock court
must have accustomed him to the practice; and yet, despite the fact
that he knows everyone at court considers him royal, he is in Chapter
VI apparently ignorant of this part of court etiquette:

> Tom was conducted to the principal apartment of a noble suite, and
> made to sit down—a thing which he was loath to do, since there were
> elderly men and men of high degree about him. He begged them to be
> seated, also, but they only bowed their thanks or murmured them, and
> remained standing. He would have insisted, but his "uncle," the Earl of
> Hertford, whispered in his ear:
> "Prithee, insist not, my lord; it is not meet that they sit in thy
> presence."

Tom's principal reaction to the elaborate ceremonials surrounding him is quite typical of Huck Finn. Hemmed in on all sides by
rules, forms, and procedures, he finally exclaims to himself, "In what
have I offended, that the good God should take me away from the
fields and the free air and the sunshine, to shut me up here and make
me a king and afflict me so?" His difficulties are in fact almost a
carbon copy of the troubles experienced by Huck at the Widow
Douglas' house.

The Prince and the Pauper is in subject and setting what Joseph
T. Goodman termed it, "a groping among the driftwood of the
Deluge,"[32] a radical departure from anything Twain had thus far
attempted. Consequently, sandwiched as it is between Tom Sawyer
and Huckleberry Finn, it appears to be an aberration, but in a study
of Twain's experiments with structure it is the necessary connecting

link between the two. Like *Tom Sawyer,* it uses for its foundation and frame a plot-outline from an early burlesque. For its basic structure, *Tom Sawyer* uses the actual condensed burlesque novel with but little change; but in *The Prince and the Pauper,* Twain, intent upon his instructive purpose, has borrowed the pattern of the burlesque *L'Homme qui rit* but not the burlesque itself. As in *Tom Sawyer,* Twain has used the plot thus gained as a narrative-plank along which he has arranged a series of episodes. Faced with a structural problem within the frame, the problem of uniting plot and theme, he found the solution in an instructive journey, thus introducing into the novel a device which, prior to this book, was characteristic of the travel narratives. Such a solution looks forward to *Huckleberry Finn* where once again, faced with a problem in structure, Twain falls back upon his travel-book techniques.

III

Of the novels written before 1885, *Huckleberry Finn* gave Twain the greatest trouble. *Tom Sawyer* and *The Prince and the Pauper* both occupied at the most about three years from idea to finished text; *Huck* was seven years and two months in the making. Its long gestation began when *Tom Sawyer* was just finished and extended beyond the completion of *The Prince and the Pauper.* During this time, it passed through at least two structural stages which together epitomize within the growth of this one novel the structural developments represented by the other two. Walter Blair has demonstrated that Twain returned to his book three different times in the seven years he took to finish it.[33] There is not enough evidence to permit a reconstruction of the structural pattern Twain was following in the first stage of composition, but enough exists to indicate that in the second and third stages he was drawing upon his experience in writing burlesque not only for the major outlines and character relationships of the novel, but also for specific episodes within the text. The second structural stage apparently followed the pattern of *Tom Sawyer*, using as its frame a burlesque detective story similar to and to some extent dependent upon *Simon Wheeler, Amateur Detective.* The novel was, evidently, undergoing expansion by the insertion into the frame of burlesque episodes borrowed from the unfinished *Autobiography of a Damn Fool,* a burlesque of temperance literature. Apparently, only in the final stages of construction did the structural pattern of the published text emerge, a pattern derived from early travel-burlesque techniques but devoid of any burlesque intent. Because the final pattern involves a parallel between a journey and the central character's struggle with his conscience, it is similar to the "moral pilgrimage" of *The Prince and the Pauper.*

According to Blair's reconstruction of Twain's work on the novel, Twain started the book in 1876, returned to it in 1879-80, and continued to add to it at various intervals between 1880 and 1883. A distinct manuscript stage is associated with each of these three periods of work: a four-hundred-page holograph manuscript representing the work of 1876, two typescripts of the work done in 1879 and 1880, and the final text as it appeared in printed form. For convenience these three manuscripts may be designated MS-I, MS-II, and MS-III.

The evidence regarding the structural pattern of MS-I is meager. In his letter to Howells on August 1, 1876, Twain describes his story as "Huck Finn's Autobiography."[34] The use of the word *autobiography* may suggest a pattern similar to that of the *Autobiography of a Damn Fool,* but Twain's working notes seem to belie such a suggestion.[35] Note B-2 shows clearly that MS-I was to some extent concerned with the death of Pap, for it contains three references to Pap's death and disappearance, the page numbers in the references indicating by their size that the citations are to the holograph manuscript: "218—the dead man is Huck's father, 223—the [dead man] again [is Huck's father], 244 more about Finn—his disappearance." The care with which Twain has noted these three references suggests that in 1879-80, when he made the notations, Pap's death was important to him in his plans for the novel, but there is no guarantee the events were of equal importance when he wrote MS-I three years earlier: they may represent details surviving from some larger structural pattern.

Enough evidence exists concerning MS-II to suggest strongly that by 1880 Twain had a completed frame for his book, one which he was obliged to abandon some time during the 1879-80 work period in favor of the pattern of the finished text, MS-III. The clearest evidence that he did actually consider himself close to the end when he was working on the MS-II material is in Note A-10, which reads, "Back a little, CHANGE—raft only *crippled* by steamer." DeVoto regards this note as evidence that "the book got tired in 1876" at the point where the steamer ran down the raft. "The destruction of the raft," he concludes, "had stopped him short; he had not known what to do with the story."[36]

But this conclusion presupposes too much lack of invention in Mark Twain. DeVoto assumes that Twain planned from the beginning to take Huck and Jim on a journey downstream to the Phelps's farm, but if such had been Twain's original intent, he would not have destroyed the raft in the first place. If in a momentary lapse he had destroyed it, he, the creator of the fictive world and all its events, would not be rendered impotent by one of his own errors. If Twain is the master of "lordly improvisation" which DeVoto declares him to be in the discussion of *Tom Sawyer,* he certainly would not require six or seven years to find a simple solution to such a minor plot problem. The destruction of the raft occupies two paragraphs; Mark Twain's manuscripts are filled with passages of a comparable length and containing similar missteps which he has struck out with no hesitation and rewritten to give his story the desired direction. The destruction of the raft was not a mistake benumbing Mark Twain's inventiveness or a symbol of his frustration, but a deliberate action in keeping with the plot he had in mind at the time he wrote this section, a plot the final scenes of which were to be acted out in conjunction with the Grangerford-Shepherdson feud. The resurrection of the raft is understandable only if one assumes that Twain had made changes in his plans for the novel.

The A notes contain other implications that Twain was at or close to the end of whatever plot he originally had in mind. Note A-1, "boys give bill of sale of Jim," furnishes two clues. The word *boys* indicates that at the time Twain wrote the note he had in mind a development requiring the presence of both Tom and Huck. The presence of Tom implies a re-establishment of communication with St. Petersburg and with it an unraveling of both Huck's and Jim's disappearances. The reference to the bill of sale suggests that control of Jim's welfare has passed from Tom and Huck to some third person. Note A-2 includes another bit of suggestive evidence: "Being in a close place, Huck boldly offers to sell Jim—the latter turns pale but dasn't speak—secretly is supported in the trial by firm belief that Huck is incapable of betraying him." Huck's offer to sell Jim, a desperate measure indeed, implies again that in Twain's planning the end is very near. However, both notes are vague; nothing very conclusive can be drawn from them.

The notation that Jim "secretly is supported in the trial by firm belief that Huck is incapable of betraying him" is of particular interest because of the phrase "in the trial." As it stands, it is ambiguous: it can refer either to the emotional trial produced by Huck's offer to sell or to an action in a court of law. Other pertinent evidence tends to shift the balance in favor of the second interpretation, that at the time of the note Twain intended his novel to culminate in a courtroom scene. *Huckleberry Finn*, as it was finally published, contains an unfinished murder plot which begins with Huck's elaborately arranged murder scene in Pap's cabin. As Huck learns when he returns to town disguised as a girl, the townspeople, suspecting both Pap and Jim of the murder, have posted rewards for both. Pap, however, has disappeared. The third day after the "murder," he "was around till after midnight with a couple of mighty hard-looking strangers, and then went off with them." Huck reports an incident of the following evening—four days after the "murder" and one day following Pap's disappearance—apparently relevant to this plot:

> By the time it was night I was pretty hungry. So when it was good
> and dark I slid out from shore before moonrise and paddled over to the
> Illinois bank—about a quarter of a mile. I went out in the woods and
> cooked a supper, and I had about made up my mind I would stay there
> all night when I hear a *plunkety-plunk, plunkety-plunk,* and says to
> myself, horses coming; and next I hear people's voices. I got everything
> into the canoe as quick as I could, and then went creeping through the
> woods to see what I could find out. I hadn't got far when I hear a
> man say:
> "We better camp here if we can find a good place; the horses is
> about beat out. Let's look around."

Huck is driven to the Illinois shore by the knowledge that some-
one else is on Jackson's Island with him; the arrival of the horsemen
serves in the final version to motivate his return to the island.[37] But
Twain has taken care to tie this event and the discovery of Jim's
campfire chronologically to Huck's "murder" and Pap's disappearance, deliberately specifying the time element: "And so for three
days and nights. No difference—just the same thing. But the next
day I went exploring around down through the island." The idea
suggests itself that the horsemen are the "couple of mighty hard-
looking strangers" in whose company Pap was last seen.[38] The discovery of Pap's body in the floating house several days later is the
last incident connected with the murder plot. After Chapter XI,
Twain makes no further reference to the whole affair until the very
end of the novel when Jim tells Huck the dead man in the house
was Pap. In making this last reference Twain has forgotten or has
chosen to ignore the fact that Jim is not only a runaway slave but
an accused murderer with a price on his head. As a result he credits
Miss Watson with a most unprecedented philanthropy when in her
will she sets Jim free.

Despite the oversight, apparently Twain still placed a relatively
great measure of importance upon Pap's murder at the time he was
working on the novel in 1879 and 1880, a fact indicated by his sec-

ond meticulous notation of references to Pap's death in the C-1 notes. The careful reviewing of the murder-plot details not once but twice and the total lack of references to Huck's conscience in these early notes suggests that the murder plot was at this time uppermost in Twain's mind. The fact that the book at this stage of development was, apparently, to culminate with the Grangerford-Shepherdson feud indicates that the murder details and the feud were to be connected in the climax of the plot.

During the gestation of *Huckleberry Finn,* Twain was much interested in murder plots and detective stories. Paine records that in the summer of 1876 Twain worked enthusiastically on his "blindfold-novelettes" project entitled "A Murder and a Marriage."[39] The following summer Twain wrote a play, *Simon Wheeler, Amateur Detective,* which he never published, but which apparently held his fancy for some time, for from 1877 to about January, 1879, he worked unsuccessfully to turn the play into a novel. Pertinent evidence indicates that his 1879-80 structural plan for *Huckleberry Finn* drew at least some of its characteristics from the *Simon Wheeler* plot.

The Simon Wheeler play is a burlesque of Allan Pinkerton's detective stories, highly fictionalized accounts of what may have been actual cases solved by Pinkerton's agency. In the play, the burlesque target is specifically named by Captain Wheeler: "B'George! when I've finished working up this case it'll be worthy a chapter in one of Allen Pinkerton's great detective books."[40] In the novel, the head of the detective agency is named Flathead, but Pinkerton is still the target: each of the three detectives, Billings, Baxter, and Bullet, wears a badge described as "a big silver disk with a staring human eye engraved upon it, surrounded by the modest legend, 'WE NEVER SLEEP' "—the insignia, that is, of Pinkerton's agency.[41] The burlesque is rather generalized, although Twain may have had in mind as a specific target the lurid tale entitled *Mississippi Outlaws and the Detectives,* a yarn filled with robberies, murder, lynching, and addlepated detective work laid in the Tennessee-Kentucky border region and featuring Island Number 10 and Reelfoot Lake, places mentioned by Twain in Group A of his notes for *Huckleberry Finn*. The plot of the play hinges on a murder which never occurred. Hugh Burnside, the village poet, believing himself spurned by his sweetheart, buys a sleeping potion with which he attempts suicide. He succeeds only in putting himself into a sound sleep for some hours. During the sleep, his "body" is found, but while the discoverers are absent, Hugh awakens and laments his failure even as a suicide. At this moment Jake Belford appears on the scene disguised as a begging Civil War veteran; Jake has committed a murder at another town farther up the Mississippi and has eluded the authorities. His disguise gives Hugh another idea: he trades clothes and equipment with Jake and, lest his voice be recognized, assumes the role of a deaf-mute. Almost immediately after the exchange of clothes, Jake is killed by a random gunshot, and once again Hugh's "body," identified by the clothes, is discovered. Hugh thus has the opportunity of watching the search for his "murderer" and of attending his own funeral.

The play has only two similarities to *Huckleberry Finn*. As a supposed murder victim, Hugh is in a position very much like that of Huck, and the tramp, Jake Belford, is the prototype of the king, although in the finished text of *Huckleberry Finn* the king is not a fugitive murderer. The play, consequently, does not appear to be very closely connected with *Huckleberry Finn*. As Blair has pointed out, a much closer connection appears in the Simon Wheeler novel:

... Twain ... had conceived of two of the characters and of the chief happening of the Grangerford-Shepherdson episode when writing the fictional version of *Simon Wheeler, Amateur Detective*. The feud in the uncompleted novel started so far back in the past that its very cause has been forgotten, yet it is a matter of honor and glory to continue it. Judge (at one time Colonel) Griswold is described and characterized in terms often identical with those used in representing Col. Grangerford. The daughter of one of the feuding families is the prototype of Sophia Grangerford, and like the delicate Sophia, she is wooed and won by a member of the clan feuding with hers.[42]

Other bits of evidence, when coupled with the similarities noted by Blair, indicate that Twain had the *Simon Wheeler* plot in mind while he was working on *Huckleberry Finn* in 1879-80. Despite his sex, Hugh Burnside, still a poet and still in love with Milly, although Milly is now a member of the opposite clan in the feud, is clearly the prototype of Emmeline Grangerford. Believing himself disappointed in love, he writes a poem comparable to any "tribute" written by Emmeline. As Twain notes, Hugh is, like Emmeline, somewhat morbid. While in the grip of the despondency which produced his poem, he says, "Flowers are a mockery. There is nothing real but the tomb." Even so, his artistic sense is ever alive; after this remark, Twain says, "He had the presence of mind to get out his note-book & set down this thought for future use in some particularly damnable poem." But, although Hugh is clearly the source for Emmeline, he is also connected with the Duke in *Huckleberry Finn*. The title of his poem, "The Crushed Heart's Farewell," is descriptive of the Duke's poem, "Yes, crush, cold world, this breaking heart."

Two other characters in *Huckleberry Finn* appear briefly in the Simon Wheeler novel. The Grangerfords' Negro woman, Betsy, is, in the earlier novel, the mother of Toby, a servant highly appreciative of Solomon's wisdom. Toby also has a brother on another plantation, a brother named Jim to whom he has caused a particularly elegant but highly inappropriate letter to be written. The letter, copied from a book of models, is one from a young lady rejecting a suitor, but when Jim receives it, he becomes the envy of all the other Negroes. Strange Negroes from distant plantations come to see him and hear the letter. The notoriety is such that Jim, like his counterpart in *Huckleberry Finn,* becomes "stuck up" and "just about ruined" as a plantation hand.

Most revealing of all, however, is the fact that Twain has borrowed directly from the Simon Wheeler novel in writing *Huckleberry Finn* and in so doing has inadvertently altered his description of Colonel Grangerford. At the beginning of Chapter XVII, when

Huck first enters the Grangerford house, Twain describes the Colonel as "gray and about sixty"; but at the beginning of the next chapter, when Twain gives a more detailed description, the Colonel is no longer gray:

Col. Grangerford was very tall and very slim, and had a darkish-paly complexion, not a sign of red in it anywheres; he was clean-shaved every morning all over his thin face, and he had the thinnest kind of lips, and the thinnest kind of nostrils, and a high nose, and heavy eyebrows, and the blackest kind of eyes, sunk so deep back that they seemed like they was looking out of caverns at you, as you may say. His forehead was high, and his hair was black and straight and hung to his shoulders.

The new conception of the colonel, borrowed directly from the Simon Wheeler novel, parallels the description of Judge Griswold: "He was sixty years old; very tall, very spare, with a long, thin, smooth-shaven intellectual face, & long black hair that lay close to his head ... & fell straight to his coat collar without a single tolerant kink or relenting curve. He had an eagle's beak & an eagle's eye."

These borrowings, taken together with the unfinished murder plot in *Huckleberry Finn,* intimate that in its early stages *Huckleberry Finn* was to be a burlesque detective story. Apparently its denouement was to feature Jim's trial for Huck's murder, a crime never committed; Pap's murder as well as the mock murder were to be connected with the Grangerford-Shepherdson feud in a plot-complex similar to that of *Simon Wheeler,* Pap's murder corresponding to the grisly crime for which Jake Belford in the *Simon Wheeler* plot is sought. The fact that Tom is to be present at least during the final episode suggests that he was to play a role similar to that of Simon Wheeler, establishing the guilt of the tramp and exonerating Jim by producing his supposed victim.[43]

However, as Note A-10, urging the resurrection of the raft, indicates, Twain found the structural plan of his second work period insufficient for some reason, possibly because it was not readily expandable. Faced with the necessity of carrying on with a story he apparently had thought was almost finished, he sought a means of adding to what he had already written. The device he adopted, as the resurrection of the raft suggests, is similar to that which solved his difficulty in *The Prince and the Pauper*: he decided to drop the culmination which would coincide with the feud and to continue Huck's journey downstream in the company of two tramp printers. In this early stage of the journey a burlesque intent is still clearly evident. Note A-5 reads in part, "The two printers deliver temp. lectures, teach dancing, elocution, feel heads, distribute tracts, preach, fiddle, doctor (quack)." The idea of taking Huck and Jim on a tour of the lower Mississippi with the tramp printers is one Twain had first devised for the *Autobiography of a Damn Fool* (1876). In the notes for this story, Twain writes, "Listens to the printer-tramp & is charmed. Goes on a months expedition in summer with him, delivering temperance lectures & sermons & spreeing on the proceeds." This is followed by the notation, "BURNING SHAME."[44] The note furnishes the hints for the two episodes with the Duke and the King which, as Blair suggests, finish the portion of the book written during the second period of work on the novel: the King's sermon at the camp-meeting and the Royal Nonesuch. The *Autobiography of a Damn Fool* is a series of burlesques of temperance tracts and kindred literature. Like Mamie Grant, the Damn Fool reads tracts and Sunday-school literature and with disastrous results tries to apply what he learns to his own life. The King's sermon at the camp-meeting is a continuation of such burlesque.

Up to this stage in the construction of the novel, there is no clear evidence that Twain meant to involve Huck in a struggle between his heart and his conscience over his aid to Jim. Several of the A and B notes show that Huck is aiding Jim and that there is a strong bond of trust between them. Note A-2 specifies that Jim has a "firm belief that Huck is incapable of betraying him." But nothing in these notes indicates that the treatment of Jim in the central portion of the book is to be any different from the comic-opera treatment of the initial and final sections. Indeed, although there are indications that Jim's trouble was to spring from the mock murder, no evidence suggests that Jim's runaway status occasioned any qualms in Huck. In fact, the state of the structural pattern during the second period of work seems to indicate that Twain never seriously considered organizing his book on the basis of Jim's plan to escape up the Ohio River. Note A-10 makes it clear that the raft was to carry Huck and Jim into the midst of the Grangerford-Shepherdson feud. Since this feud, either as the Darnell-Watson feud, the Burnside-Griswold feud, or the Grangerford-Shepherdson feud, is consistently associated with the vicinity of Island Number 10 and Reelfoot Lake in the Kentucky-Tennessee border region, it is unlikely that in the early stages of *Huckleberry Finn* Twain moved it upstream beyond Cairo. Indeed, the various references to Island Number 10 and Reelfoot Lake in the A notes show clearly that even before the destruction of the raft Twain had taken his characters past Cairo, that is, past the logical turning-off point for a runaway slave seeking free territory. He would have no objections to such a move if the primary consideration were to involve Jim, a suspected murderer, in just such a murder plot as that suggested by the evidence; but if the primary aim were to take Jim to freedom, such a move is ridiculous.

The first clear reference to Jim as a runaway slave appears in Chapter III of *Life on the Mississippi,* where as an introduction to the raftsman's episode Twain summarizes the first portion of *Huckleberry Finn:*

The book is a story which details some passages in the life of an ignorant village boy, Huck Finn, son of the town drunkard of my time out West, there. He has run away from his persecuting father, and from a persecuting good widow who wishes to make a nice, truth-telling, respectable boy of him; and with him a slave of the widow's has also escaped. They have found a fragment of a lumber raft..., and are floating down the river by night, and hiding in the willows by day— bound for Cairo, whence the negro will seek freedom in the heart of the free states. But, in a fog, they pass Cairo without knowing it.

Notably lacking from the summary and from the raftsman's chapter itself is any reference to Huck's moral dilemma. Yet the details make it clear that the chapter was excised from a point in the text close to Huck's first attack of conscience in Chapter XVI, evidently immediately after it.[45] The most reasonable inference to be drawn from these circumstances is that Huck's moral problem did not form a part of Twain's plans for the novel at the time he was writing *Life on the Mississippi* in 1883.

The evidence indicates, then, that the structural principle of the great middle section of the novel was not added until Twain was working on MS-III. The new pattern, firmly based upon the successful patterns of *Roughing It* and the middle section of *The Prince and the Pauper,* appears in epitome in Chapter XXXI when Huck debates with his conscience and finally decides "All right, then, I'll *go* to hell." Clearly the journey downriver with Jim is designed to provide "no places to harden [Huck] against him." In giving this epitome, Twain repeats the procedure he followed in the opening chapter of *Roughing It* and in the initial interview between Edward and Tom Canty in *The Prince and the Pauper.* The journey itself, then, is closely connected with and parallel to the essential matter of the book: it is not Jim's journey in search of freedom but Huck's journey, during which, as Twain described it ten years later, a sound heart collides with a distorted conscience and gains the victory.[46]

The shift to the new plan would imply the necessity of extensive revisions and expansions of MS-II. A comparison of page references in the Group C notes, the review notes of MS-II, with the corresponding points in MS-III shows that major additions were indeed made. Note C-1 contains the reference "Jim has wife & 2 children.—90." If Blair's calculation of 336 words a page in MS-II is correct,[47] ninety pages of MS-II contain 30,240 words, whereas in MS-III the total to this point is 36,630 words after due allowance for the *Walter Scott* insert. Twain added, then, nearly 6,400 words, almost one-fifth the MS-II total to this point. To learn specifically what was added with these 6,400 words is impossible, but the existence of such major revisions suggests that Twain went back over the earlier manuscript, superimposing upon his text the necessary preparation for the newly conceived plan.

With the change in design, the unmistakable characteristics of the travel narratives begin to appear, much more clearly than in *The Prince and the Pauper.* In the finished text the relationship between Huck and Jim is a curiously complex matter. Insofar as Huck's conscious morality and humanity are concerned, Jim is Huck's tutor, setting an example with his simple dignity and eliciting from Huck a response which transcends the bounds of color. But mingled with this human bond is a relationship analogous to the Mr. Twain–Mr. Brown character-axis. Chapter XIV, containing the discussion of Solomon and the French language, owes a substantial debt in its conception to the relation of traveler and companion in the travel-burlesque. This chapter is a late addition to the novel: a part of the *Walter Scott* insert, its pagination in the Buffalo Public Library manuscript shows that it was added to MS-III.

The idea for the passage first appears in note C-4 as a proposed change: "Back yonder, Huck reads & tells about monarchies & kings &c. So Jim stares when he learns the rank of these two." The establishment of a relationship between Huck and Jim similar to the burlesque character-axis coincides with the change in structural plan from murder plot to journey. For the occasion Huck assumes a role having much in common with that of the refined traveler, a role which places him in the tradition of Mr. Twain, the tenderfoot of *Roughing It,* and the narrator of *A Tramp Abroad.* During the argument about Solomon's wisdom, Huck stubbornly holds his ground, his opinion firmly rooted in the books he has read and the story told by the Widow Douglas. Jim, like Mr. Brown, refuses to accept these authorities and persists in examining the matter in the light of his own reason. Like Mr. Twain, who tells Brown the "santipedes" and other insects are "trifles," Huck is forced to exclaim, "But hang it, Jim, you've clean missed the point—blame it, you've missed it a thousand mile." But like Brown, who claims a scorpion's bite is no trifle, Jim is unimpressed: "Doan' talk to *me* 'bout yo' pints. I reck'n

I knows sense when I sees it; en dey ain' no sense in sich doin's as dat." Just as Mr. Twain finds no use in trying to reason with "that fellow Brown," so Huck concludes: "I never see such a nigger. If he got a notion in his head once, there warn't no getting it out again. He was the most down on Solomon of any nigger I ever see."

In view of Huck's attainments or lack of them in *Tom Sawyer* and in the first twelve or thirteen chapters of *Huckleberry Finn,* it is surprising to learn he has suddenly reached that stage of refinement which permits him to discuss the French language and even to speak and translate a bit. But as the refined traveler of *The Innocents Abroad* knows, a smattering of French is one of the sure signs of refinement and culture. Jim's reaction to Huck's French is quite similar to that of the Sinner, who finds, after listening to the Italians, that "foreigners always spell better than they pronounce." This discussion ends, as did the one about Solomon, with Huck, defeated by Jim's lack of refinement, remarking, "I see it warn't no use wasting words—you can't learn a nigger to argue. So I quit." The temporary distortion in the characterization of Huck and Jim can best be accounted for by assuming that Mark Twain was momentarily too much under the influence of the pattern he had used in earlier narratives; the implication is that, in making the transition to a new over-all narrative plan, he was seizing upon expedients.

Twain has used the character-axis not only with Huck and Jim but with the other major figures as well; as a consequence characters appear in pairs: Tom and Huck, Huck and Jim, the Duke and the King, and finally Tom and Huck again. In each pair, the first member has to a greater or lesser degree characteristics traceable to Mr. Twain, while the second member exhibits those of Mr. Brown. For example, the Twain-Brown relationship is almost fully developed between the Duke and the King. When these two first come aboard the raft, their relative positions in the character-axis appear in their speech. When the Duke reveals his "true" estate, his language abounds in the clichés of historical romance; in his initial speech on the subject he even resorts to alliteration: "To think I should have lived to be leading such a life, and be degraded down into such company." In describing his present lot among men, he manages to employ almost as many hackneyed phrases as Mr. Twain does when he views the valley of bones in the Sandwich Islands: "...I am the lineal descendant of that infant—I am the rightful Duke of Bridgewater; and here am I, forlorn, torn from my high estate, hunted of men, despised by the cold world, ragged, worn, heartbroken, and degraded to the companionship of felons on a raft!" And again, when he is forced to take the shuck bed, he says, " 'Tis my fate to be always ground into the mire under the iron heel of oppression. Misfortune has broken my once haughty spirit; I yield, I submit; 'tis my fate. I am alone in the world—let me suffer; I can bear it."

In contrast to his almost elaborately stylized language, the King's speech is vernacular in the extreme. To the Duke's alliterative speech, the King replies, "Dern your skin, ain't the company good enough for you?" After the Duke lays his "poor broken heart" to rest, the King exclaims, "Drot your pore broken heart...; what are you heaving your pore broken heart at *us* f'r? *We* hain't done nothing." In the matter of the shuck bed, the King says, "I should 'a' reckoned the difference in rank would a sejested to you that a corn-shuck bed warn't just fitten for me to sleep on. Your Grace'll take the shuck bed yourself." Each of the Duke's refined speeches is thus balanced by one of the King's unrefined speeches, indicating a deliberate attempt on Twain's part to establish a character-axis between these two on the basis of their linguistic habits. But the surest evidence of the Duke's refinement is his ability to write sentimental poetry. From the title, "Yes, crush, cold world, this breaking heart," the poem presumably is just as effective an emetic as those Mr. Twain quotes to Mr. Brown on the Sandwich Islands journey.

When the King assumes his role as Peter Wilks's brother, the contrast between his pretensions and his language results in a verbal chaos reminding the reader of the "Oracle" in *The Innocents Abroad*. Like the "Oracle," who placed both "Pillows of Herkewls" on the same side of the Straits of Gibraltar and then invented a list of "authorities" to prove his contention, the King confuses *orgies* and *obsequies* and, when the Duke corrects him, invents an etymology:

"I say orgies, not because it's the common term, because it ain't— obsequies bein' the common term—but because orgies is the right term. Obsequies ain't used in England no more now—it's gone out. We say orgies now in England. Orgies is better, because it means the thing you're after more exact. It's a word that's made up out'n the Greek *orgo,* outside, open, abroad; and the Hebrew *jeesum,* to plant, cover up; hence in*ter.* So, you see, funeral orgies is an open er public funeral."

By treating his major characters in pairs and modeling each pair on the Twain-Brown axis, Twain has produced a major contradiction in Huck, whose orientation on the axis shifts toward one end or the other as he moves from relationship to relationship. When he is with Tom, he plays the role of Brown to Tom's Mr. Twain. In the discussion about jinn, Huck is as impervious to Tom's arguments as Jim is to his in the discussion about Solomon. After Tom explains the duties of a jinni, Huck replies, "Well, . . . I think they are a pack of flatheads for not keeping the palace themselves 'stead of fooling them away like that. And what's more—if I was one of them I would see a man in Jericho before I would drop my business and come to him for the rubbing of an old tin lamp." When Tom argues that he would have to come, Huck's reply is one which Jim would understand and appreciate: "What! and I as high as a tree and as big as a church? All right, then; I *would* come; but I lay I'd make that man climb the highest tree there was in the country." The reply provokes from Tom an estimate of Huck's mental abilities which is the same as Huck's estimate of Jim's at the conclusion of the Solomon discussion: "Shucks, it ain't no use to talk to you, Huck Finn. You don't seem to know anything, somehow—perfect saphead." In the latter portion of the book, Tom reaches the same conclusion after the discussion of plans for Jim's escape: "It ain't no use to try to learn you nothing, Huck."

By placing two of these character pairs together on the raft, Twain has achieved a set of relationships more complex than anything he had yet attempted. In the society on the raft, the two pairs, the Duke and the King on the one hand and Huck and Jim on the other, function as units in a relationship similar to that which exists between the two members of each pair. As Huck takes his place alongside Jim in the Brown-oriented pair in this new character-axis, the small measure of refinement which separates him from Jim suffers a slight degeneration. His new position is most clearly indicated by his sudden and inexplicable ignorance about the forms of address suitable for nobility. At the outset of the Solomon discussion, he explains how he acquired the knowledge which permits him to assume the role of authority on the authorities in relation to Jim: "I read considerable to Jim about kings and dukes and earls and such, and how gaudy they dressed, and how much style they put on, and called each other your majesty, and your grace, and your lordship, and so on, 'stead of mister; and Jim's eyes bugged out, and he was interested." Huck knows how nobility should be addressed, but when the Duke asks that Huck, Jim, and the King show him the respect due his rank, Huck as well as Jim needs instruction:

Jim pitied him ever so much, and so did I. We tried to comfort him, but he said it warn't much use, he couldn't be much comforted; said if we was a mind to acknowledge him, that would do him more good than most anything else; so we said we would, if he would tell us how. He said we ought to bow when we spoke to him, and say "Your Grace," or "My Lord," or "Your Lordship"—and he wouldn't mind it if we called him plain "Bridgewater," which, he said, was a title anyway, and not a name; and one of us ought to wait on him at dinner, and do any little thing for him he wanted done.

Similarly, Huck's eyes are as wide as Jim's when first the Duke and then the Dauphin announce their "true" identities. Nevertheless, Huck is more knowledgeable than Jim in the matter of dukes and kings. Jim accepts the two frauds at their face value, but true to the test of his own observation he reaches a sound conclusion about their worth: "But, Huck, dese kings o' ourn is reglar rapscallions; dat's jist what dey is; dey's reglar rapscallions." His perception is acute enough to distinguish the difference between the Duke and the King: "Now de duke, he's a tolerble likely man in some ways." Huck reaches the same conclusion about the other pair on the raft, and like Jim he perceives the relative merits of the two. Unlike Jim, he does not accept the Duke and the King at their face value: "It didn't take me long to make up my mind that these liars warn't no kings nor dukes at all, but just low-down humbugs and frauds." But, despite the fact that both Huck and Jim reach the same conclusions about the other pair, Huck still retains his own level in relation to Jim. Jim is surprised that his observation reveals kings and dukes to be rapscallions. Huck is not: for one thing, he knows this pair to be frauds; for another, his "authorities" have convinced him that "all kings is mostly rapscallions, as fur as I can make out." To illustrate his point he gives Jim a lecture about Henry VIII. He finds little to choose between the frauds at hand and the "reality" of his books. Consequently he reaches Jim's conclusion, but by a means consonant with his own position in relation to Jim.

Twain's experience in writing burlesque has guided him not only in the major outlines and character relationships of the finished novel, but also in the use of specific burlesque episodes within the text. The targets of these episodes have been rather thoroughly explored and catalogued; consequently there is little point in reviewing the matter once again.[48] It is more important to notice that in their use Twain has to some extent departed from his previous patterns with important consequences in the characterization of Huck.

In *Huckleberry Finn,* as in *Roughing It,* the greatest number of passages influenced by Twain's earlier training in burlesque foreshadow "real" events to follow. Tom Sawyer's gang, built upon the romance of banditry, prefigures the bandits trapped on the *Walter Scott.* The important cohesive element in Tom's gang is honor and respect for the oath, "a real beautiful oath," partly Tom's invention, but for the most part gleaned from "pirate-books and robber-books."

As Tom says, ". . . every gang that was high-toned had it." The oath

> swore every boy to stick to the band, and never tell any of the secrets. . . .
> And if anybody that belonged to the band told the secrets, he must
> have his throat cut, and then have his carcass burnt up and the ashes
> scattered all around, and his name blotted off the list with blood and
> never mentioned again by the gang, but have a curse put on it and be
> forgot forever.

Clearly Twain intends the reader to have Tom's conception of
banditry in mind when Huck boards the *Walter Scott*. At the outset
of the episode, Huck twice refers to Tom. In the debate with Jim
about landing on the wreck, Huck culminates his argument with a
description of Tom's probable attitude toward such an opportunity.
Again, when he first hears the three criminals arguing, he screws up
his courage by saying, "Tom Sawyer wouldn't back out now, and so
I won't either; I'm a-going to see what's going on here." He discovers
a robber gang involved in settling just such a case of betrayal as
Tom's oath was intended to dispose of.

The implied burlesque of temperance literature in the new
judge's attempt to reform Pap is a prelude to Pap's drunken denun-
ciation of the government and his bout with delirium tremens. Similarly, as several critics have pointed out, the burlesque discussion
of Solomon, the French language, and finally the Dauphin serves
as an introduction for the Duke and the King. In the same fashion,
the burlesque pathos in the drawings and poetry of Emmeline
Grangerford introduces the tragedy of her family in the last bloody
outburst of the feud. In addition, the burlesque titles of her pictures
furnish the first clue which labels the Duke as a fraud. Fond of the
word *alas,* Emmeline uses it to end each picture title: "Shall I Never
See Thee More Alas," "I Shall Never Hear Thy Sweet Chirrup More
Alas," and "And Art Thou Gone Yes Thou Art Gone Alas." The
Duke's first word in his role as rightful heir to the rank and estate
of Bridgewater is "Alas!" and it appears several times more as the
two frauds adjust themselves in their new roles. The only major bur-

lesque episode which does not introduce a serious event of a similar nature is the escape plot at the end. It reverses the pattern followed previously; that is, it follows Huck's escape from Pap and Jim's escape from Miss Watson with a burlesque of escape literature. The repetition of the burlesque-serious contrast throughout the book, too frequent to be accidental, indicates that Twain was deliberately using in this novel the alternation of serious and comic passages for which he strove in his travel books and which he described in his letters to Livy and Mrs. Fairbanks.

In subject, then, these passages have a certain appropriateness in relation to the other matter of the book. They differ, however, from similar passages in previous books in that few, if any, of them are concerned with the development of Huck's character. In *Roughing It* such sections represent the beliefs of the young tenderfoot who views his projected trip West through the "mellow moonshine of romance." In effect he is a structural device because his mind is the medium through which the burlesques are introduced into the text. Huck's mind produces only two burlesque passages, the Solomon discussion and the lecture on Henry VIII and the morals of kings. The others, although to a greater or lesser degree concerned with Huck, do not spring from him or his expectations. None of them, except in a most general fashion, contribute to his moral or mental growth. For example, although he participates in Tom's gang and for a while believes Tom's fiction, he is free of his illusions long before he boards the *Walter Scott*. He could see no profit in running around and charging upon hog-drivers and women in carts without taking anything, and he is unable to perceive Tom's Arabs and diamonds in a Sunday-school picnic. After trying hard but unsuccessfully to produce a jinni from an old tin lamp, he concludes "that all that stuff was only just one of Tom Sawyer's lies." In none of these burlesque-serious contrasts does the "reality" force him to readjust a book-inspired notion. Even the contact with the Duke and King fails to produce a readjustment of his ideas about the aristocracy because, instead of contradicting what he has learned from his reading, they confirm his notions even though he knows the two are frauds.

Although none of the burlesque passages contributes directly to Huck's development, all but one of them, the final escape burlesque, serve an important function in relation to Huck. They not only foreshadow "real" events to follow but also furnish a necessary contrast to the "real" events, a contrast between the false and the true in the fictive world which makes an important contribution to Huck's verisimilitude. The eager blood-thirst of Tom Sawyer's gang is the only standard in the fictive world by which the reader can measure Huck's reaction to the fate of the robbers on the *Walter Scott*. As a result of the false note, Huck's concern for the robbers has a truer ring. Similarly, the reader has only the effusions of Emmeline Grangerford by which to measure Huck's reaction to the deaths of Buck and the others. All Huck says is "I cried a little when I was covering up Buck's face, for he was mighty good to me." The emotional impact of the single sentence—the reader's conviction about the depth of Huck's feeling—results to a great extent from the contrast between his tribute and those written by Emmeline Grangerford. Finally, the false religiosity of the King, first revealed in the camp-meeting burlesque of reform literature, is the prelude to Huck's agonizing search for an answer to his moral problem. Thus the majority of these passages form a pattern not only of burlesque followed by serious but also of the false in sentiment followed by the real of the fictive world, with a resultant deepening of the reader's insight into Huck's character. The burlesques, then, are pertinent to the central problem of the book, that is to Twain's theme of a sound heart in conflict with a deformed conscience. They are illustrative of those moral and social principles which Huck's deformed conscience, derived from Miss Watson's lectures on Providence, labels good. The burlesque tone carries Twain's implicit judgment of the code against which he pits Huck's heart. As a consequence he is able to avoid the necessity of any explicit statements from Huck on the question of right and wrong which would be dissonant with Huck's limited ability to verbalize abstract concepts and which, as a result, would destroy the basic irony derived from Huck's conscious conviction that what he is doing on Jim's behalf is morally wrong.

The only section which does not follow, indeed which reverses, the previous pattern is the escape burlesque at the end, the subject of much critical discussion. Twain himself thought highly of it, apparently letting his enthusiasm for burlesque outweigh all other considerations. When he used it for public reading, he wrote to Livy from Pittsburgh, on December 29, 1884:

Well, mamma, dear, the child is born. To-night I read the new piece—the piece which Clara Spaulding's impassibility dashed & destroyed months ago—& it's the biggest card I've got in my whole repertoire. I always thought so. It went a-booming; & Cable's praises are not merely loud, they are boisterous. Says its literary quality is high & fine —& great; its truth to boy nature unchallengeable; its humor constant & delightful; & its dramatic close full of stir & boom, & *go*. Well, he has stated it very correctly.[49]

So far as the Evasion alone is concerned, Twain is right. To read it without laughing is difficult, and Twain's delivery on the lecture platform undoubtedly made it even more hilarious. Nevertheless, the entire final section represents an admission of defeat in the attempt to give the book a coherent form. The book is essentially a structural failure because the travelers reach no physical goal in their journey, and during the Evasion Huck fails to act in accordance with the instinctive humanity which characterizes his relations with Jim during the journey.

The notes of 1883 show that Twain was struggling with the problem of ending the physical journey. C-4 contains the notation "& Jim can be smuggled north on a ship?—no, steamboat," with the phrase *& Jim can be smuggled north* crossed out. Presumably the return northward to the end of the journey was to be accomplished, following the defeat of Huck's deformed conscience, with a dispatch comparable to Prince Edward's return from Hendon

Hall to Westminster Abbey and the throne. But Twain apparently could not work out a plot device which would permit the return; instead, he reintroduced Tom, in a sense bringing the end of the journey to Huck and Jim, and embarked upon an extended burlesque of escape literature.

Nor, apparently, could he work out a conclusion consonant with Huck's triumphant heart and the prevailing comic tone of the novel. In the critical debate about the concluding section, Leo Marx sums up the majority opinion when he says that the reader is "forced to put aside many of the mature emotions evoked earlier" by the events on the raft. He does not object to "the inclusion of low comedy per se" and recognizes the place of humor "even in works of high seriousness." In *Huckleberry Finn,* however, he says "the case differs from most . . . : the major characters themselves are forced to play low comedy roles."[50] His assumption is that Huck and Jim are not comic characters but figures cast in roles of high seriousness, but a heavy role is not congenial to either Huck or Jim. Comic characters, derivatives to some extent of burlesque characters, both have their moments of high seriousness, but moments only in the encompassing comedy. Nor can the Evasion be dismissed on the grounds of improbability, for the world in which Huck and Jim live is one in which the laws of probability have been suspended, even to the extent that their raft is miraculously resurrected the moment Huck needs transportation away from the Grangerfords' plantation. In such a world the extravagance of the Evasion is just as normal as the feud, the robbers quarreling over their loot on the sunken *Walter Scott,* and the murder of Boggs by Colonel Sherburn.

And yet, even if Huck's and Jim's participation in the comedy of the final section cannot be charged off as a flaw, Lionel Trilling is correct when he says, "Certainly this episode is too long . . . and certainly it is a falling-off."[51] Any perceptive reader is conscious of a distinct disappointment the moment Tom appears on the scene and the escape plot gets under way. Marx touches upon one of the reasons when he writes, "Moreover, the serious motive in the novel,

Jim's yearning for freedom, is made the object of nonsense."[52] But Marx is in error when he assumes that Jim's desire for freedom is "the serious motive" of the book. Jim and his desire are merely the objects about which Huck's dilemma has centered and for which Huck has decided to go to hell. It is instead Huck's loyalty, his heart, which becomes submerged in the nonsense of the Evasion despite Twain's frequent efforts to salvage it. If the reader accepts, as he must, the initial premise of the book, that it is narrated after the events of the journey have transpired, that as in *Roughing It* the pronoun "I" used by the narrator links two different characters, the irresolute boy of the earlier stages of the journey and the self-committed friend of the latter, the assumptions with which he approaches the Evasion are totally disappointed.

In Chapter XV, the reader is led to assume that Huck's humanity will eventually govern all his actions in relation to Jim. After Huck tricks Jim into believing that the separation in the fog was a dream, after Jim tells him that "trash is what people is dat puts dirt on de head er dey fren's en makes 'em ashamed," Huck says, "It was fifteen minutes before I could work myself up to go and humble myself to a nigger; but I done it, and I warn't ever sorry for it afterward, neither. I didn't do him no more mean tricks, and I wouldn't done that one if I'd 'a' knowed it would make him feel that way." The explicit promise made here is broken during the Evasion; the reader is disposed to regard it as a succession of mean tricks, but Huck is almost totally unaware that his actions are analogous to his earlier joke.

Trilling defends the "certain formal aptness" of the ending principally because he believes "some device is needed to permit Huck to return to his anonymity, to give up the role of hero."[53] But part of the reader's disappointment in the conclusion is precisely the fact that Huck does withdraw to a subordinate role in the plot to free Jim. A large portion of the book's charm rests in the fact that Huck and Jim, by hook or more often by crook (and sometimes with the aid of a particularly co-operative Providence), always manage to squirm out of their difficulties. The reader's expectation is disappointed when Tom reappears and Huck almost too meekly permits himself to be shouldered out of the way. To be consistent with the pattern of lesser evasions successfully engineered earlier, the conclusion should feature an escape brought about principally by Huck and Jim themselves with the aid of a miraculous Providence, if necessary. But, since the Evasion denies the two basic assumptions fostered earlier by the structural pattern, the book as a whole must be judged a structural failure, despite the fact that it is Twain's masterpiece, undoubtedly great in many other respects. /

5

Conclusion

THE RECORD of Mark Twain's work from the beginning of his career to 1885 is one of constant struggle and achievement in structure. Yet Twain himself has been responsible for fostering the myth that he was totally unconcerned about structure. In his *Autobiography* he included a passage written in Florence, in 1904, which has become almost the scriptural text for all discussions of his plots; portions of it have been quoted so often to the wrong end that it is well to review the whole:

Within the last eight or ten years I have made several attempts to do the autobiography in one way or another with a pen, but the result was not satisfactory; it was too literary. With the pen in one's hand, narrative is a difficult art; narrative should flow as flows the brook down through the hills and the leafy woodlands, its course changed by every bowlder it comes across and by every grass-clad gravelly spur that projects into its path; its surface broken, but its course not stayed by rocks and gravel on the bottom in the shoal places; a brook that never goes straight for a minute, but *goes,* and goes briskly, sometimes ungrammatically and sometimes fetching a horseshoe three-quarters of a mile around, and at the end of the circuit flowing within a yard of the path it traversed an hour before; but always *going,* and always following at least one law, always loyal to that law, the law of *narrative,* which *has no law.* Nothing to do but make the trip; the how of it is not important, so that the trip is made.

With a pen in the hand the narrative stream is a canal; it moves slowly, smoothly, decorously, sleepily, it has no blemish except that it is all blemish. It is too literary, too prim, too nice; the gait and style and movement are not suited to narrative. That canal stream is always reflective; it is its nature, it can't help it. Its slick shiny surface is interested in everything it passes along the banks—cows, foliage, flowers, everything. And so it wastes a lot of time in reflections.[1]

The passage, in part or in whole, has been cited time and again as proof that Mark Twain preferred a loose, rambling form for everything he wrote. G. W. Feinstein, for example, quotes it and concludes, "He opposes a studied perfection of plot, favors instead a loose, spontaneous development of narrative." The conclusion in turn leads Feinstein to say, "Mark Twain values, not the architectonic effect of a tale, but the art of the paragraph, the sentence, the illuminating incident."[2]

But such critics as Feinstein forget that this passage refers to the *Autobiography*. Mark Twain specifies its application to the *Autobiography* at the beginning of the passage and again in the "Author's Note" preceding this section of the book:

Finally in Florence, in 1904, I hit upon the right way to do an Autobiography: Start it at no particular time of your life; wander at your free will all over your life; talk only about the thing which interests you for the moment; drop it the moment its interest threatens to pale, and turn your talk upon the new and more interesting thing that has intruded itself into your mind meantime.[3]

Furthermore, the success of such a narrative plan depends upon dictation. Twice he charges himself, as a writer, with the very architectonic sense the statement supposedly proves he lacked. The passage begins, "Within the last eight or ten years I have made several attempts to do the autobiography in one way or another with a pen, but the result was not satisfactory; it was too literary." Within the passage, he says, "With a pen in the hand the narrative stream is a canal; it moves slowly, smoothly, decorously, sleepily, it has no blemish except that it is all blemish. It is too literary, too prim, too nice." In other words, Twain's difficulty with the *Autobiography* was that when he sat down to write, his architectonic sense got in the way. Inevitably, he would have the reader believe, the result of his writing was too structured, a neatly and sharply delineated canal; he had to search and struggle for "eight or ten years" to find a way to avoid such a structured result.

Twain has left very few statements about his own methods in writing novels, but one of the most revealing is recorded by Brander Matthews. In the summer of 1890 he described to Matthews his method of work in the writing of *Tom Sawyer* and *Huckleberry Finn*:

He began the composition of *Tom Sawyer* with certain of his boyish recollections in mind, writing on and on until he utilized them all, whereupon he put his manuscript aside and ceased to think about it, except in so far as he might recall from time to time, and more or less unconsciously, other recollections of those early days. Sooner or later he would return to his work to make use of memories he had recaptured in the interval. After he had harvested this second crop, he again put his work away, certain that in time he would be able to call back other scenes and other situations. When at last he became convinced that he had made his profit out of every possible reminiscence, he went over what he had written with great care, adjusting the several instalments one to the other, sometimes transposing a chapter or two and sometimes writing into the earlier chapter the necessary preparation for adventures in the later chapters unforeseen when he was engaged in the beginnings of the book. Thus he was enabled to bestow on the completed story a more obvious coherence than his haphazard procedure would otherwise have attained.[4]

The last portion of the passage is extremely important and should be written in italics, for it bespeaks a great concern on Twain's part for structure. It is doubly important because the record of Mark Twain's struggle with the problem of structure in the period under consideration attests to its accuracy.

Between 1863 and 1884, Twain developed from his apprenticeship in burlesque a distinctive structural technique. The basis of Twain's structure in any of his fictive works in this period is what he called the "narrative-plank." In the travel books, it derives from the fictional antagonism between two travelers who entertain mutually exclusive views upon the various events of a journey; in the novels prior to *Huckleberry Finn,* it is a plot or idea gained from one of his condensed burlesques. In *Huckleberry Finn* it is once again the conjunction of two characters on a journey. The use of the burlesque plots as the basis of *Tom Sawyer* and *The Prince and the Pauper* is another instance of that dependence upon ideas in other works of fiction to which Twain confessed on several occasions. To account for some of this dependence, he evolved a theory of "unconscious plagiarism." In a letter to Howells in 1875 he wrote, "I would not wonder if I am the worst literary thief in the world, without knowing it."[5] Much of his borrowing undoubtedly was unconscious, for Twain was a man with a retentive memory who read widely on all levels of fiction. But that borrowing which is rooted in his burlesques was, of necessity, conscious. To such deliberate borrowing Twain has also confessed. Blair describes an unpublished portion of a letter written in 1876 in which such a confession is made.[6] Since the ideas only are borrowed, the result is nothing like the originals when Twain has completed the transplantation, for they become in his hands mere foundations upon which he rears a structure of episode, character-axis, and theme all his own.

Because the episode was to Twain an important ingredient of the novel, that "narrative-plank" which permitted the insertion of the greatest possible number of episodes was the best. For this reason he frequently resorted to a journey as the solution of his structural problems. The episode furnishes variety and interest, keeps the story from becoming an essay. From St. Louis on January 10, 1885, he sent to Livy a copy of a letter written to a beginning writer:

I have read the story, & it has merit, but not enough to enable me to say the *strong* word necessary to rouse a publisher's interest & desire. I should have to be straightforward with him, & tell him the truth: that it is a moral essay, & an earnest & heartfelt essay, but more an essay than a story. And I should have to say ... that incidents & episodes &

situations are hardly frequent enough, & when they occur are not successfully handled.[7]

The episodes should not, however, be disconnected. In "Fenimore Cooper's Literary Offences," the second of the nineteen rules of romantic fiction is "that the episodes of a tale shall be necessary parts of the tale, and shall help to develop it." Brander Matthews attests that Twain "went over what he had written with great care," making certain that his episodes were related one to the other and to the tale as a whole. Indeed, a careful scrutiny of Twain's three novels in the period under discussion reveals the care expended upon this aspect of structure. A search for episodes which can be deleted without destroying some connection with another results in the discovery of only three or four such episodes in three full-length novels.

From the beginning of his career, Twain strove for an alternation between comic and serious material in the arrangement of the episodes, relying to a large extent upon burlesque to furnish the comedy. Gradually he refined his use of the burlesque material to the point where it not only furnished an alternation with the serious material but in conjunction with it furnished foreshadowing and, as a consequence, thematic unity. Thus in *Roughing It* burlesques constitute the tenderfoot's prevision of the West and a foreshadowing of the disillusioning experiences which are to follow. A similar pattern is visible in *Huckleberry Finn*. Twain's readiness to use burlesque was a source not only of strength but also of weakness, for, accustomed to seek in burlesque answers to structural problems, he produced, for example, the incongruous Evasion to end his greatest novel.

The frequent use of burlesque both for the "narrative-plank" and for episodes forces a re-examination of Twain's position as a "realist." Twain was fond of saying that in *Tom Sawyer* and *Huckleberry Finn* there was no episode which did not grow out of his own boyhood experiences and in *Roughing It* no episode which did not stem from his own adventures in the West. Such statements have led critics like Edgar H. Goold to assume that Twain demanded in fiction a reportorial representation of actual personal experience. Goold reviews several such statements by Twain and concludes, "The theories of fiction writing discussed so far are clearly those of the realist in matters of technique."[8] But a writer's stated theories of art do not necessarily govern his practice of it. Mark Twain does not in practice seek to achieve reportorial accuracy in fictional representation either in the novel as a whole or in the individual episodes. His very willingness, or perhaps one may say eagerness, to include burlesque demonstrates this. Furthermore, Twain has been quite explicit on the point. In a notebook entry, quoted by Goold, Twain planned an article for the *Princeton Review*:

For Princeton Review—to be written in April, 1888: If you attempt to create a wholly imaginary incident, adventure or situation, you will go astray, and the artificiality of the thing will be detectable, but if you found on a *fact* in your personal experience it is an acorn, a root, and every created adornment that grows up out of it, and spreads its foliage and blossoms to the sun will seem reality, not inventions. You will not be likely to go astray; your compass of fact is there to keep you on the right course.[9]

Twain does not claim that the finished incident in the story is a fact in one's personal experience; he says that the fact is "an acorn, a root" upon which the "created adornment" grows to hide the fact under a spreading and blossoming foliage of invention. The aim is to produce a seeming reality, not to reproduce actuality.

Inevitably discussions of Twain's "realism" must touch upon the question of probability. Goold, for example, states, "A cardinal rule of Mark Twain's for the fiction writer was that he should stick to probabilities."[10] But one is forced to ask, Is it probable that two people, floating down the Mississippi, will meet with all the adventures Huck and Jim encountered? The answer can only be in the negative. Goold bases his conclusion upon two statements by Twain. At the head of Chapter XV of *Following the Equator*, "Pudd'nhead Wilson's New Calendar" includes the remark, "Truth is stranger than fiction, but it is because Fiction is obliged to stick to possibilities; Truth isn't." The ninth rule for the writing of romantic fiction in "Fenimore Cooper's Literary Offences" is "that the personages of a tale shall confine themselves to possibilities and let miracles alone; or, if they venture a miracle, the author must so plausibly set it forth as to make it look possible and reasonable." In a note, Goold says, "Although Clemens usually uses the term 'possibilities,' it is clear from his remarks that 'probabilities' would have been more exact."[11] But Goold forgets the thirteenth rule for the writing of fiction: "Use the right word, not its second cousin." If Mark Twain can be trusted on anything, he can be trusted on his choice of words. A novel which draws its plot from a burlesque is not going to be very probable; in fact, it is quite likely to be beyond the bounds of the possible. Mark Twain frequently ventures upon the miraculous, but he follows his ninth rule and sets the miracles forth so plausibly that they look possible and reasonable within the fictive world he has created for them. In speaking of Twain's "lordly improvisations," DeVoto says of *Tom Sawyer*, "It cannot be thought of as comprehensive or profound realism."[12] With a suitable modification of the word *profound*, the same must be said in regard to *Huckleberry Finn*.

Largely as a justification for the introduction of burlesque episodes, Twain drew from the conventions of the Dr. Syntax travel-burlesques two distinctive character-types, one or both of which appear in one form or another in all his works of this period. One is a person whose view of life is molded by concepts gleaned primarily from picturesque travel literature or sentimental fiction; the other is "a bitter enemy of sentiment." Many of the burlesque episodes, especially those in *Tom Sawyer* and *Huckleberry Finn*, are debates between two such characters, the one quoting his "authorities" on the right way of doing certain things, the other subjecting those "authorities" to the test of his own common sense and finding them lacking. The relationship between these two characters, what I have called the Twain-Brown character-axis, becomes a vehicle for a series of burlesque episodes and thus may be called a structural device as well as a means of characterization. Out of the character-axis grew Twain's first "developing" character and, finally, his most memorable. In *Roughing It* Twain conceived the idea of educating his refined traveler by placing him in situations which would reveal to him the absurdity of those "authorities" in which he had placed his trust. The "moral pilgrimage" is but an extension of this type of developing character, and Huck is a derivative, consequently, of the tenderfoot in *Roughing It.*

Theme, which to Twain frequently signified *moral,* early became an important ingredient in the making of a novel. Criticism and literary history have tended to date his first attempt in the "serious and instructive" vein with *The Prince and the Pauper.* But the evidence afforded by the burlesque *L'Homme qui rit* establishes his interest in theme a full decade earlier. Each of the three novels of this period has its instructive vein. The antislavery thesis which has its roots in the abortive allegory of the Hugo burlesque runs through *The Prince and the Pauper* and *Huckleberry Finn* to *A Connecticut Yankee. Tom Sawyer,* the first full-length novel of Twain's own making, is the only one of the period with a distinctly different theme. As Blair has pointed out, a portion of the book is devoted to a reversal of the model-boy theme of current Sunday-school literature. The end of this reversal is the affirmation that morality is not the peculiar property of model boys. The didactic vein of *Tom Sawyer* is, however, weak and tentative, possibly because Twain had not yet discovered a method by which he could merge theme, plot, and character. By the end of the period, he had worked out a means which evidently suited him. Building upon the device first used in *Roughing It*, Twain conceived the idea of taking his character on a journey during the course of which the character encounters a series of adventures forcing upon him a realization of a moral truth. The device, the "moral pilgrimage," is first used almost tentatively in *The Prince and the Pauper*, but in *Huckleberry Finn* an adaptation of it becomes the narrative-plank and thus the central structural device.

Huckleberry Finn marks the end of the first period of structural experimentation, and, because Twain tried to make the journey the frame of the novel, it ends the period with an impasse. Twain himself must have recognized that he had worked himself into an untenable position because in his next novel, *A Connecticut Yankee*, he abandoned the structure of *Huckleberry Finn* and reverted to a pattern which combines that of *Tom Sawyer* with that of *The Prince and the Pauper*. *A Connecticut Yankee* employs what is basically a burlesque of the Arthurian legend as its narrative-plank and as its central episode sends Arthur and Sir Boss on a moral pilgrimage quite comparable to that of Prince Edward and Miles Hendon.

Huckleberry Finn, then, is the culmination of a long period in which Twain evolved a highly complex structural technique. It is not at all accurate to say, as Andrews says, "Its greatness cannot be attributed to conscious skill and its success testifies not to art but to instinct."[13] Nor is it accurate to say, as DeVoto says, of Mark Twain as craftsman, "He had little ability to impose structure on his material; he could not think and feel it through to its own implicit form."[14] He did indeed think his material through; he struggled to find the proper form. Critics may disagree with Twain on the suitability of the form he chose and suggest other forms they consider better, but Twain sought for and found the form he thought best. Late in his life, Twain said:

There are some books that refuse to be written. They stand their ground year after year and will not be persuaded. It isn't because the book is not there and worth being written—it is only because the right form for the story does not present itself. There is only one right form for a story, and if you fail to find that form the story will not tell itself.[15]

Huckleberry Finn stood its ground for almost seven years, but finally, by drawing upon techniques gleaned from his burlesque apprenticeship and perfected during twenty years of writing, Mark Twain found what was for him and his story the right form. Mark Twain's masterpiece is the result of long deliberation and careful craftsmanship.

Notes

CHAPTER 1

1. Albert Bigelow Paine, *Mark Twain, A Biography* (New York: Harper & Bros., 1912), (hereafter *Biography*), II, 610.

2. *Ibid.*, pp. 670-71.

3. *Ibid.*, p. 890.

4. Gladys C. Bellamy, *Mark Twain as a Literary Artist* (Norman: University of Oklahoma Press, 1950), p. 136.

5. *Ibid.*, pp. 95-96.

6. Edgar M. Branch, *The Literary Apprenticeship of Mark Twain* (Urbana: University of Illinois Press, 1950), pp. 93-94.

7. Vernon L. Parrington, *Main Currents in American Thought* (New York: Harcourt, Brace & Co., 1930), III, 91-92.

8. *Ibid.*, pp. 94-95.

9. Van Wyck Brooks, *The Ordeal of Mark Twain* (New York: Meridian Books, 1955), p. 182.

10. *Ibid.*, pp. 94-95.

11. Bernard DeVoto, *Mark Twain's America* (Boston: Little, Brown & Co., 1932), p. 225.

12. *Ibid.*, p. 241.

13. *Vanity Fair*, IV (November 30, 1861), 245.

14. Despite the somewhat arbitrary definitions of the words *burlesque* and *parody* given in the preface to this volume, the reader should bear in mind that the nineteenth-century humorists made little, if any, distinction in meaning between the two terms and frequently used them synonymously.

15. Bayard Taylor, *The Echo Club and Other Literary Diversions* (Boston: James R. Osgood, 1876), p. 64.

CHAPTER 2

1. Dixon Wecter, *Sam Clemens of Hannibal* (Boston: Houghton Mifflin Co., 1952), p. 209.

2. For a detailed study of the history and conventions of the burlesque novel,

see Archibald B. Shepperson, *The Novel in Motley* (Cambridge: Harvard University Press, 1936).

3. For a discussion of the burlesques appearing in *Vanity Fair* and especially of the contributions of Kerr and Ward, see Walter Blair, "Burlesques in Nineteenth-Century American Humor," *American Literature* (hereafter *AL*), II (November, 1930), 236-47.

4. Unpublished letter, typescript in Mark Twain Papers, University of California Library, Berkeley (hereafter MTP).

5. Evans is the Fitz Smythe to whom Twain makes frequent references in this period. For details of the Evans-Twain rivalry, see *Mark Twain: San Francisco Correspondent*, ed. Henry Nash Smith and Frederick Anderson (San Francisco: Book Club of California, 1957), pp. 17-38.

6. To his mother and sister, *Mark Twain's Letters*, ed. A. B. Paine (hereafter *Letters*) (New York: Harper & Bros., c. 1917), I, 101.

7. "The Jumping Frog" sketch so violently repudiated in this letter is usually cited as the finest example of Twain's frontier humor. The history of his attitude toward the sketch reveals the gradual abandonment of his Bohemian urbanity as he realized, more or less consciously, that his role as "Wild Humorist of the Pacific Slope" was his best literary asset in the East. Apparently he took almost four years to change his mind about the story. In a letter to Livy on March 1, 1869, he is still convinced that the sketch is vulgar, but not as bad as *Don Quixote*: "Read nothing that is not *perfectly* pure. I had rather you read fifty 'Jumping Frogs' than one Don Quixote" (*The Love Letters of Mark Twain*, ed. Dixon Wecter [New York: Harper & Bros., 1949], p. 76). On December 14, 1869, he wrote to Livy, "...A man might tell that Jumping Frog story fifty times without knowing *how* to tell it—but between you & I, privately Livy dear, it is the best humorous sketch America has produced, yet, & I must read it in public some day, in order that people may know what there is in it" (*Love Letters*, p. 41). The "villainous backwoods sketch" has become "the best humorous sketch" in America, but he still has not brought himself to use it before the public. He speaks "privately" to Livy about his belief and puts off any public presentation to a vague "some day." Shortly after this letter he came to care enough about it to sacrifice his friendship with Webb in order to secure an unclouded title to it. On January 22, 1870, he wrote Bliss that he was "prosecuting Webb in the N. Y. Courts—think the result will be that he will yield up the copyright & plates of the Jumping Frog, if I let him off from paying me money" (*Mark Twain to Mrs. Fairbanks*, ed. Dixon Wecter [San Marino: Huntington Library, 1949], p. 144, n. 1). In the final settlement with Webb, Twain paid $1,400. The settlement came just after Twain contracted with Bliss to write *Roughing It* (*Mark Twain to Mrs. Fairbanks*, pp. 143-44).

The change in attitude toward the sketch is a complete reversal of the change Van Wyck Brooks and his followers believe took place when Twain moved from San Francisco to the East. In the period which saw the beginning of his friendship with Mrs. Fairbanks, his engagement and marriage to Livy, and his first association with the Reverend Mr. Twichell, he was sloughing off much of the pose of sophistication cultivated during his Bohemian days in San Francisco and beginning to capitalize upon his role as an "old-timer" in the "wild" West.

8. Typescript of Notebook 4-5, Part III, pp. 46-52, MTP. The burlesque was written about September, 1866, immediately after the return from Hawaii.

9. Typescript of Notebook 6, pp. 37-41, MTP.

10. Typescript of Notebook 10, pp. 1-9, MTP.

11. *Letters*, I, 182-83.

12. *Mark Twain: San Francisco Correspondent*, pp. 116-17.

13. Charles Henry Webb, *Parodies in Prose and Verse* (New York: G. W. Carleton, 1876), pp. 30, 33, and *John Paul's Book* (Hartford: Columbian Book Co., 1874), pp. 416-18.

14. A careful distinction between the type of word game Webb plays in *St. Twel'mo* and the malapropism is necessary and important. Mrs. Malaprop knows the meaning of the word she wants and has a vague notion of its general phonetic shape. Her uncertainty about the pronunciation produces a word phonetically similar but totally dissimilar in meaning. For example, when she wants the word *alligator,* she blurts out *allegories.* Little Etna, on the other hand, has no notion of the meaning of the word or its fitness in the context, but she has mastered the pronunciation.

15. *Mark Twain of the Enterprise*, ed. Henry Nash Smith (Berkeley: University of California Press, 1957), pp. 36-38, 94.

16. The use of this style as an index to Twain's burlesque intent is complicated by the fact that he also used it seriously. In the description of Honolulu Harbor the burlesque nature of the passage, suggested by the style, is confirmed by the dispute between Mr. Twain and Mr. Brown which follows. The same style appears in the description of Kilauea Volcano in which, devoid of burlesque intent, Twain is obviously striving to impress his readers with the awesome grandeur of the scene.

17. Unpublished letter, original in MTP.

CHAPTER 3

1. *Love Letters*, pp. 165-66.

2. *Mark Twain to Mrs. Fairbanks*, p. 227.

3. Collected and edited by Charles Honce, the series was republished in 1928 under the title *The Adventures of Thomas Jefferson Snodgrass.*

4. Throughout the discussion of the Sandwich Islands Letters, *Mr. Twain* will refer to the fictive narrator; *Twain* or *Mark Twain* to the author.

5. *Letters from the Sandwich Islands,* ed. G. Ezra Dane (Palo Alto: Stanford University Press, 1938), p. 49.

6. William Combe's bibliography is in a chaotic state, but apparently the Dr. Syntax tours were quite popular. Between 1821 and 1868 at least ten

English editions or reprintings appeared. Natalie and Bon of London published an unnumbered edition or printing in 1868.

7. William Combe, *Doctor Syntax's Three Tours* (London: John Camden Hotten, 1868), p. 41.

8. *Ibid.*, p. 7.

9. These brief paragraphs no more than sketch Combe's influence on subsequent nineteenth-century travel-burlesque. For further information on Dr. Syntax's effect upon the *Pickwick Papers*, see Wilhelm Dibelius, "Zu den *Pickwick Papers*," *Anglia*, XXXV (1912), 101-10. Dibelius also lists a few other works in the Syntax tradition of travel-burlesque. The *Pickwick Papers* themselves fostered a respectable progeny, in numbers at least: *The Pickwick Gazette* (1837), *Pickwick Abroad; or, The Tour of France* by G. W. M. Reynolds (1837-38), *The Post-humourous Notes of the Pickwickian Club* in two volumes (1839?), *Pickwick in America!* by "Bos" (1840), and *Pickwick in India* (1840). William Thomas Thomas, under the pseudonym W. T. Moncrieff, wrote *Sam Weller's Tour; or, The Pickwickians in France,* a play based on Reynolds' spurious sequel.

The staff of *Punch* returned to the type at almost regular intervals. A few of the titles are "Punch's Continental Tour" (begins October 14, 1843), "Travels in London" (begins November 2, 1847), and "Our Tourist in Paris" (begins September 3, 1853). Perhaps the worst travel-burlesque to be found is "The Telegraph Tour of Broadway Spuytentuyfel and His Cousin Peytona Randolf de Accomac," which begins in the June 30, 1860, issue of *Vanity Fair.* Less well-known than Dickens' or Thackeray's work but considerably better than the "Telegraph Tour" is J. Ross Browne's *Yusef* (1853). The unfinished series "Boston as Viewed by Mr. Peeps," beginning in *Vanity Fair*, June 20, 1863, is of interest because the pseudonymous Mr. Peeps appears, from the evidence of style, to be Charles Henry Webb.

Interestingly enough, Hugh Henry Brackenridge anticipated the nineteenth-century travel-burlesque with his own independent adaptation of *Don Quixote* in *Modern Chivalry* (1792-1815). The relationship between Captain Farrago and Teague Oregan is quite similar to that of the refined traveler and his companion.

10. The close parallel between the glove-buying episode in *The Innocents Abroad* (I, 108-12) and a similar episode in the adventures of Jack Easel (*Punch,* February 2, 1861, p. 43) suggests that Twain had read the Easel series, or portions of it at least.

11. In 1864 Burke and Prescott, newsdealers in Virginia City, were offering subscriptions to almost all English periodicals at reasonable rates and were guaranteeing delivery by mail as far as the Reese River mining frontier. See *Washoe Herald,* July 2, 1864, p. 4.

12. *Letters from the Sandwich Islands,* pp. 191-92.

13. *Ibid.*, p. 22.

14. Printed October 17, 1866.

15. Leon T. Dickinson, "Mark Twain's *Innocents Abroad:* Its Origins, Composition and Popularity" (unpublished dissertation, University of Chicago, 1945), pp. 92-95.

16. Twain was still joking about Hugo's novel four months later. In his letter dated April 19, he describes his troubles with the porter at his hotel. When requested to bring reading material, the porter brought, among other things, a copy of the novel. Twain comments: "I shall never cease to admire the tact and intelligence of that gifted porter. I moved to the Tepfer House next day." The episode was used in *The Innocents Abroad,* II, 401-3.

17. The first edition appeared in 1853. Twain probably used the second edition of 1861 published by M. Doolady of New York, for in the preface to the second edition Wight says the first "has long been out of print."

18. *The Innocents Abroad,* I, 193.

19. *Petri Abaelardi Opera,* ed. Victor Cousin, C. Jourdain, et E. Despois (Paris: A. Durand, 1849-59), I, 10.

20. François Guizot, *Abaelard et Héloïse* (Paris: Didier et Cie, 1876), p. 53.

21. Valléry Gréard, *Lettres complètes d'Abélard et d'Héloïse* (Paris: Garnier Frères, 1870), p. 11.

22. O. W. Wight, *Lives and Letters of Abelard and Heloise* (2d ed.; New York: M. Doolady, 1861), p. 99.

23. *Ibid.,* p. 96.

24. *Ibid.,* pp. 99-100.

25. The legend was originally published in the *Overland Monthly,* I (October, 1868), 316-20.

26. The indebtedness to Thackeray shows that Twain had improved upon his Bohemian tutors, Webb and Harte, by turning directly to the originator of the condensed-novel form.

27. George C. D. Odell, *Annals of the New York Stage* (New York: Columbia University Press, 1927-49), VIII, 495, 499, 636, 665.

28. The word *zampillaerostation* has long since disappeared from the vocabulary of troupers and theater-goers, but at the time of the *Quaker City* voyage it reflected the introduction of a new and thrilling acrobatic performance: "This elongated word was coined by James Lingard, the manager of the Bowery Theatre, New York, and simply means a performance on the flying trapeze. The grace and dash of Mr. Hanlon in this wonderful act, which was then entirely new, created a marked sensation at the time. As no net was used beneath the trapeze, the danger was much greater than nowadays" (Eugene Tompkins, *History of the Boston Theatre 1854-1901,* p. 92).

29. Dickinson, *op. cit.,* p. 109 and n. 6.

30. For a list of the deletions see Dickinson, *op. cit.,* Appendix G9, pp. 206-9.

31. Although the reporter was in actuality E. H. House, in the *Alta* letter he should be regarded as a fictional character.

32. The extent of the actual conflict appears best in the paragraph beginning "As advertised, the 'Plymouth Collection of Hymns' was used on board." Appar-

ently the cause of most of the recriminations, it was deleted in the final section of *The Innocents Abroad,* "A Newspaper Valedictory." Innocuous enough to the modern reader, the paragraph nevertheless would provoke comment from the passengers of the *Quaker City,* for it is a satirical attack upon one of the passengers, Bloodgood H. Cutter, the "Poet Lariat." Twain's comment, "There were those in the ship's company who attributed the fact that we had a steady siege of storms and head winds for five mortal months solely to the prayer meetings," and the subsequent remarks about prayer meetings are ironic sallies at Cutter, who, in incredibly bad verses, attributed the bad weather to the dancing on shipboard:

> I thought on Monday how some danced,
> And round on deck how many pranced;
> And it doth seem that since that day
> Boisterous and rough has been our way.

> To thus dance on the ocean waves,
> Seems like frolicking o'er our graves;
> For my own part don't it approve,
> To condemn it now my pen doth move.

("The 'Quaker City' Excursion," *The Long Island Farmer's Poems,* p. 19).

33. *The Innocents Abroad,* I, 143-44.

34. *The Innocents Abroad,* II, 425-27. The reporter is rather sensitive about his notebook entries, so much so that he has rewritten and greatly expanded the one he quotes. In the actual notebook, the only entry concerning the trip by sea from Alexandria to Gibraltar is the one for October 11, a meager entry indeed:

Oct. 11—At sea, somewhere in the neighborhood of Malta. Very stormy.

Terrible death—to be talked to death

The storm has blown two small land birds & a hawk to sea & they came on board.

Sea full of flying fish. [Typescript of Notebook 8, p. 58, MTP]

In the finished text, he introduces his spurious notebook quotation with the comment, "We were all lazy and satisfied, now, as the meager entries in my note-book (that sure index, to me, of my condition,) prove. What a stupid thing a note-book gets to be at sea, any way." Then follow nearly two weeks of daily notes, many entries quite extensive, the only two at all related to the actual notebook entries being the fourth and fifth, which illustrate the expansion Twain has made of his original.

The entire section of spurious notebook entries reveals fully the difficulties to be encountered in the reading of the whole book. Mark Twain wanted a meager notebook quotation to show how "lazy and satisfied" his narrator and the others were, but he was unwilling to permit his readers to see just how meager his entries actually were. Within this series of entries, the Sinner has inserted four, those for Friday, Saturday, Sunday, and Monday, solely as preparation for the joke to be given on the next page with the quotation from his boyhood journal.

35. The reporter is not always so clear-eyed. At times he becomes almost indistinguishable from the refined traveler, not only covering things up "with a woof of glittering sentences," but also quoting poetry:

We had such glimpses of the Rhone gliding along between its grassy banks; of cosy cottages buried in flowers and shrubbery; of quaint old red-tiled villages with mossy mediaeval cathedrals looming out of their midst; of wooded hills with ivy-grown towers and turrets of feudal castles projecting above the foliage; such glimpses of Paradise, it seemed to us, such visions of fabled fairy-land! We knew, then, what the poet meant, when he sang of—
"—thy cornfields green, and sunny vines,
O pleasant land of France!" [*The Innocents Abroad,* I, 148-49]

The writer of this passage is the Twain who rearranged the Sandwich Islands letters to achieve a climax with the description of Kilauea Volcano and who expanded his notebook entries before exposing them to public view.

36. The book is *Rome: Its Churches, Its Charities, and Its Schools,* published by Dunigan and Brothers.

37. Twain is quoting from William C. Prime, *Tent Life in the Holy Land* (New York: Harper & Bros., 1865). He tries to conceal the source, for reasons of "taste," by changing the author's name to William C. Grimes and the title to *Nomadic Life in Palestine* (see *The Innocents Abroad,* II, 300). But he slips later and writes in a footnote, "The thought is Mr. Prime's, not mine, and is full of good sense. I borrowed it from his 'Tent Life' " (*The Innocents Abroad,* II, 344). For a fuller discussion of Twain's use of Prime's book, see Dickinson, *op. cit.,* pp. 78-80.

38. Henry Nash Smith, "Mark Twain as an Interpreter of the Far West: The Structure of *Roughing It*" in *The Frontier in Perspective,* ed. Walker D. Wyman and Clifton B. Kroeber (Madison: University of Wisconsin Press, 1957), p. 212.

39. *Ibid.,* p. 214.

40. Twain's reference to the Bowery Theater productions must be based on hearsay. Only two plays produced at the Bowery before the publication of *Roughing It* match the description: *Far West, or The Bounding Fawn of the Prairies,* produced November 14, 1870, and *Nick of the Woods,* produced November 17, 1870, both adaptations for the stage by J. J. McCloskey (T. Allston Brown, *A History of the New York Stage* [New York: Dodd, Mead & Co.,

1903], I, 147). Twain may have seen one or both of these plays during the summer tours of 1871; but he did not see them at the Bowery, for he was in Buffalo during Livy's serious illness following the birth of Langdon on November 7, 1870. Most probably he heard of them when he was in New York from December 9 to 16, 1870, seeing his *Burlesque Autobiography* through the press (*Letters*, I, 179).

41. This descriptive phrase was used on the cover of the English copyright edition of 1872, pictorial board issue; the cover bore on the left the inscription, "Showing/ How a/ Three Month's/ Pleasure Trip/ Was/ Extended to/ a Term/ of/ Seven Years," and on the right, "With a Relation/ of Many/ Humorous/ and Instructive/ Incidents/ Connected with/ the Education/ of an/ Innocent."

42. The passage summarizes, with the exception of the Sandwich Islands journey, Twain's own trip and suggests that his original intention was to use the early *Alta California* letters, those covering his trip from San Francisco to New York and to Hannibal, to complete the book. But these letters, after the deletion of the numerous local references, would not furnish sufficient material to fill out two volumes. The Sandwich Islands letters, however, offered ample wordage, even after drastic cuts. With time running out, he was apparently forced to take the easiest path out of his difficulty.

43. For a detailed bibliography of such sportsman-chronicles and an analysis of their effect upon popular and literary concepts of the West, see Earl Pomeroy, *In Search of the Golden West* (New York: Alfred A. Knopf, 1957), pp. 73-111.

44. J. Ross Browne, *A Dangerous Journey* (Palo Alto: A. Lites Press, 1950), p. 30. This and the other astonishing adventures reported by Browne supposedly occurred while he was traveling from San Francisco to San Luis Obispo, an actual trip he made in August, 1849, in his official capacity as Inspector of Postal Service. The book, therefore, is an excellent example of the literature under discussion, illustrating as it does the ease with which a factual record of experiences in the Far West drifts into fantastic romance.

45. Bénédict Révoil, *Shooting and Fishing in the Rivers, Prairies, and Backwoods of North America*, trans. The Chronicler (London: Tinsley Bros., 1865), I, 239-40. Révoil's own escape from the bear and the Comanches immediately follows this episode.

46. *Ibid.*, p. 74.

47. "My Bloody Massacre," *Sketches New and Old*, pp. 322-23.

48. The present route of U.S. 50 between Dayton and Silver Springs, Nevada, follows the old direct route across the Twenty-Six Mile Desert. Silver Springs is close to but northwest of the site of Honey Lake Smith's which is now covered by the waters of Lahontan Reservoir.

49. Albert Johannsen doubts that "Francis Johnson" is Gerstäcker's pseudonym, but considers it the name of a plagiarist (*The House of Beadle and Adams* [Norman: University of Oklahoma Press, 1950], II, 117). A traveler of some renown and a prolific writer, Gerstäcker came to the United States in 1837. He lived as a silversmith in Cincinnati, worked a farm in Missouri, held

various jobs on Mississippi river boats, and settled for two or three years at Little Rock, Arkansas. Between 1849 and 1852, he traveled around the world, visiting California during the gold rush and traveling from San Francisco to Honolulu. In 1867 and 1868 he again visited the Mississippi Valley region and traveled overland to San Francisco. As even this brief account of Gerstäcker's travels indicates, Twain must have crossed his trail several times. Out of these travels came a few factual accounts and an immense amount of fanciful romance.

50. See Johannsen, *op. cit.*, I, 132-35.

51. Franklin R. Rogers, "Washoe's First Literary Journal," *California Historical Society Quarterly*, XXXVI (December, 1957), 365-70.

52. Franklin Walker, *San Francisco's Literary Frontier* (New York: Alfred A. Knopf, 1939), p. 133.

53. *Mark Twain of the Enterprise*, pp. 138-58.

54. Rogers, *op. cit.*, p. 367.

55. The composite burlesque presented as the serial novel in the *Occidental* affords additional evidence of Twain's continuing interest in the burlesque movement in the British humor magazines. The first of such composite burlesques was announced in *Fun*, August 29, 1863. According to the notice, the next issue would commence a novel, each chapter written by a different "author." The title of this work is *Philip Dombey, The Scalp Hunter's Roundabout Secret Legacy*, by "every eminent writer of the day." The next issue, however, contains not the first instalment but further plans for the novel. The "authors" are now organized into "The London Joint-Stock Novel Company, Ltd.," and, as one would expect from the title, "Captain Mayne Reid" is to write the first chapter. The September 12 issue presents a list of all "contributors" and a discussion of the various authors' opposing and divergent views on how to proceed with the story. The novel gets under way in the first issue of Vol. V, September 19, 1863. The most famous of these composite burlesques is that announced in *Punch*, March 7, 1868: *Chikken Hazzard* (Charles Reade's *Foul Play*), written by the "Sensation Novel Company, Ltd.," including parody-burlesques of such authors as Charles Reade, Dickens, W. E. Suter, Julia Kavanagh, Wilkie Collins, and Eugène Sue.

56. *Letters*, I, 339.

57. *Ibid*, p. 349.

58. *Mark Twain to Mrs. Fairbanks*, pp. 225-26.

59. *Biography*, II, 650.

60. An American edition, *Black Forest Stories*, was published in New York by Leypoldt and Holt in 1869.

61. Kenneth R. Andrews, *Nook Farm, Mark Twain's Hartford Circle* (Cambridge: Harvard University Press, 1950), p. 290.

62. The legend which Twain calls "The Undying Head" is called "Mishemokwa" by Schoolcraft and appears on pp. 142 ff. of Schoolcraft's volume.

63. The complete title of Disturnell's book is rather imposing: *Sailing on the Great Lakes and Rivers of America; Embracing a Description of Lakes Erie,*

Huron, Michigan & Superior, and Rivers St. Mary, St. Clair, Detroit, Niagara & St. Lawrence; also, the Copper, Iron and Silver Region of Lake Superior, Commerce of the Lakes, &c. Together with Notices of the Rivers Mississippi, Missouri and Red River of the North; Cities, Villages and Objects of Interest. Forming altogether a Complete Guide to the Upper Lakes, Upper Mississippi, Upper Missouri, &c. also, Railroad and Steamboat Routes (Philadelphia: J. Disturnell, 1874).

    64. *Life on the Mississippi,* p. 437.

    65. Disturnell, *op. cit.,* p. 223.

    66. "Sketches on the Upper Mississippi," by the author of "Three Weeks in Cuba," *Harper's New Monthly Magazine,* VII (July, 1853), 182.

CHAPTER 4

    1. "Mark Twain's Part in *The Gilded Age," AL,* VIII (January, 1937), 445-47.

    2. Published by Royal Cortissoz in *Life of Whitelaw Reid* (New York: Charles Scribner's Sons, 1921), p. 273.

    3. *Mark Twain to Mrs. Fairbanks,* pp. 170-71.

    4. *Love Letters,* pp. 182-83. Miss Woolson is Constance Fenimore Woolson, grand-niece of James Fenimore Cooper, a writer of local-color stories and novels about her native Ohio.

    5. The description appears in Chapter VI. Presumably, then, from what Twain writes in his letter, Warner wrote his version during the early stages of the collaboration. The plagiarism was not discovered until the period of revision, when Warner again failed in a new attempt and Twain's description was finally inserted.

    6. Bernard A. DeVoto, *Mark Twain at Work* (Cambridge: Harvard University Press, 1942), pp. 7-8.

    7. "Mamie Grant" appears in Typescript of Notebook 10, pp. 1-9, MTP.

    8. "The Boy's Manuscript" appears in DeVoto's *Mark Twain at Work,* pp. 25 ff.

    9. *David Copperfield,* Modern Library College Editions, p. 416.

    10. Unpublished letter, MTP.

    11. Walter Blair, "The French Revolution and *Huckleberry Finn," Modern Philology,* LV (August, 1957), 22, n. 16.

    12. Henry W. Fischer, *Abroad with Mark Twain and Eugene Field* (New York: N. L. Brown, 1922), p. 60.

    13. *Biography,* I, 353.

    14. See *Mark Twain of the Enterprise,* pp. 131-32. Because no Carson City papers for the period have survived, it is impossible to establish conclusively that *Jack the Giant Killer* was performed, but in San Francisco "Toodles-Night" started with "the Nursery Fairy Burlesque of *Jack the Giant Killer"* and concluded with "the never-to-be-forgotten Toodles" (see Maguire Opera House

advertisements, *Alta California,* November 8 through 11, 1863). According to the *Alta,* the "Nursery Fairy Burlesque" was one of Marsh's more successful pieces; it is difficult, therefore, to believe that Marsh would drop it from his repertory. *Toodles* apparently impressed Twain very much. As late as 1877 it was still in his mind. In a stage direction for *Simon Wheeler, Amateur Detective,* he writes, "Always ... the Capt. must *play* sailor while in this costume. He must throw his quid into his hat & put it under his arm, hitch up his trousers with both fore-arms, trip himself up, doing it like Toodles, &c." (unpublished MS., MTP).

15. DeVoto, p. 7.

16. Walter Blair, "On the Structure of *Tom Sawyer,*" *Modern Philology,* XXXVII (August, 1939), 82-83.

17. *Letters,* I, 258 and 272.

18. DeVoto, *Mark Twain at Work,* p. 13.

19. *Ibid.,* pp. 18-19.

20. *Letters,* II, 477.

21. *Mark Twain's Notebook,* ed. A. B. Paine (hereafter *Notebook*) (New York: Harper & Bros., 1935), p. 129.

22. According to Paine's account, Twain's interest in Edward VI began with his discovery of Charlotte M. Yonge's *The Prince and the Page* in the Quarry Farm library; but as Paine points out, the two stories have little in common except that they both deal with Edward VI (*Biography,* II, 597 and note). Howard G. Baetzhold contends that Harriet Martineau's *Little Duke* was the source ("Mark Twain's *The Prince and the Pauper,*" *Notes and Queries,* I, n.s. [September, 1954], 401-3), but the only clear indebtedness he can find is in the coronation scene. Neither the *Little Duke* nor *The Prince and the Page* offers any hints as to his source for the total structure of the novel.

23. Unpublished MS., Paine No. 56, MTP.

24. Victor Hugo, *The Man Who Laughs,* trans. William Young (New York: D. Appleton & Co., 1869), p. 251.

25. *Ibid.,* p. 314.

26. *Ibid.,* p. 289.

27. *Ibid.,* pp. 248-49.

28. *Ibid.,* p. 251.

29. *Ibid.,* p. 304. Possibly the idea of exchanged identities came not from the hint in *L'Homme qui rit* but from Hugo's play *Ruy Blas,* the ultimate source of Miles Hendon, whom Twain introduces in his novel as "a sort of Don Caesar de Bazan in dress, aspect, and bearing," Don Caesar is, in *Ruy Blas,* one of the principals in an exchange of identities. He and Ruy Blas, a valet, resemble each other to such an extent that the one may masquerade as the other, a fact which Don Salluste turns to account in his plot against Donna Maria by deporting Don Caesar and introducing Ruy Blas at court in his place. Ruy Blas's impersonation parallels Tom Canty's masquerade as Prince of Wales and later as King Edward VI.

Although little evidence exists to show Mark Twain's acquaintance with *Ruy Blas,* he was well acquainted with another play, *Don Caesar de Bazan,* based upon *Ruy Blas.* He knew of *Don Caesar* as early as 1857, for he refers to it in the first Snodgrass letter (*The Adventures of Thomas Jefferson Snodgrass,* ed. Charles Honce [Chicago: Pascal Covici, 1928], p. 14). In the 1870's he had the opportunity to renew his acquaintance through his friendship with Dion Boucicault and Edwin Booth, who in 1877 toured the East with a repertory including both *Ruy Blas* and Boucicault's popular translation of *Don Caesar* (Odell, *op. cit.,* X, 204, 205, 217, 324, 366, 403, 577). One must assume that Twain saw *Don Caesar* during the period when he was working on *The Prince and the Pauper* or that the earlier experience with the play impressed itself deeply on his mind, for Twain's novel owes a substantial debt to the play. In character and appearance, Miles Hendon is drawn directly from the play; in addition, Miles's protection of Edward from the threatening crowd and his submission to a whipping in order to save Edward from the same fate are both based upon incidents in the play.

30. *Mark Twain in Eruption,* ed. Bernard DeVoto (New York: Harper & Bros., 1940), pp. 197-98.

31. It is noteworthy that Hugo uses London Bridge in the same manner in *L'Homme qui rit* both when Gwynplaine crosses it to become a lord and when he returns defeated from the House of Lords. Each time, Hugo comments upon the bridge as a symbol of the two divisions in Gwynplaine's life and character.

32. Letter to Twain, October 24, 1881, MTP; published in part in Andrews, *op. cit.,* p. 192.

33. Walter Blair, "When Was *Huckleberry Finn* Written?" *AL,* XXX (March, 1958), 1-25. I wish to acknowledge Mr. Blair's kindness in permitting me to see this article in manuscript.

34. *Letters,* I, 282-83.

35. The importance of these working notes was first recognized by Bernard DeVoto, who arranged them in three groups, A, B, and C, and published them in *Mark Twain at Work,* pp. 63 ff.

36. *Mark Twain at Work,* p. 62.

37. Logically, it is difficult to see why Huck should return to Jackson's Island under the circumstances. His most natural movement would be to avoid both the island and this spot on the Illinois shore by dropping downstream in his canoe to another hiding place.

38. Several circumstances about these travelers serve to arouse the reader's suspicions. The reference to the state of the horses indicates the men have been riding hard—good horsemen do not run their horses without due cause—in the extremely difficult brush and marsh along the riverbank, apparently preferring this route to the established north-south road a mile or so farther inland. Furthermore, these two prefer to camp out in the bottom land instead of crossing the ferry to St. Petersburg and lodging at the hotel. Of course, they may not have the price of lodgings, but even so the ordinary traveler would at least

seek congenial company at the store next to the ferry slip on the Illinois shore.

39. *Biography*, II, 578-79.

40. Unpublished MS., DV321, MTP. The first series of Pinkerton's stories was published in 1874-76 by Keen, Cooke, & Co. of Chicago.

41. Details and quotations from the Simon Wheeler novel are from the unpublished MS. in the Henry W. and Albert A. Berg Collection, New York Public Library. I am grateful to John D. Gordon, Curator of the Berg Collection, for permission to use the microfilm copy of the MS. in the MTP.

42. Blair, "When Was *Huckleberry Finn* Written?" *AL*, XXX (March, 1958), 12.

43. Because the Burnside-Griswold feud of the Simon Wheeler novel (1877-79) furnishes the major outlines and several details of the Grangerford-Shepherdson feud and predates by four years the Darnell-Watson material used in *Life on the Mississippi*, the argument is no longer valid that Twain was dependent in *Huckleberry Finn* upon the Darnell-Watson notes gathered when he revisited the river in 1883. One must conclude that the Darnell-Watson notes afforded Twain additional details which he used in MS-III to revise and expand his earlier version of the feud. Various bits of evidence suggest that *Tom Sawyer, Detective*, published in 1896, is connected with the same complex of murder plots visible in MS-II. Jake Phillips, the fugitive in this story, wears the same disguise which Jake Belford uses and is involved in a conflict with his accomplices that parallels the situation on the *Walter Scott* in which a Jake Packard is the principal.

44. Unpublished MS., DV310, MTP.

45. Bernard DeVoto inserted the section after the second paragraph of Chapter XVI when he edited the text for the Limited Editions Club (New York, 1942) and preserved this arrangement in *The Portable Mark Twain* (New York: Viking Press, 1946). In Appendix A of the Houghton Mifflin Riverside Edition, Henry Nash Smith says the raft passage "must have come originally" at this point. But a careful study of the details in the raftsman's section and the final version of Chapter XVI reveals no clear evidence to support DeVoto's placement. Indeed the details seem to suggest a placement after the attack of conscience, if one assumes the attack of conscience was in the text prior to the deletion of the raftsman's section. On the raft, Huck overhears Ed's remark that "if you take the Mississippi on a rise when the Ohio is low, you'll find a wide band of clear water all the way down the east side of the Mississippi for a hundred mile or more, and the minute you get out a quarter of a mile from shore and pass the line, it is all thick and yaller the rest of the way across" (*The Portable Mark Twain*, p. 298). Ed's information is clearly intended to provide Huck with the knowledge he later uses to discover that he and Jim have already passed Cairo. The discovery comes two days after the attack of conscience. As soon as daylight comes on the second morning, he sees "the clear Ohio water inshore, sure enough, and outside was the old regular Muddy! So it was all up with Cairo." On the previous morning, which, according to DeVoto's

arrangement, would be the morning after the visit to the raft, Huck unaccountably took no notice of the water. The conclusion must be that the raftsman's episode occurred on the night following the attack of conscience.

46. Typescript of Notebook 28a, I, p. 35, MTP. Henry Nash Smith, who first called my attention to this entry, discusses its implications more fully in his introduction to the Houghton Mifflin Riverside Edition. I wish to thank Mr. Smith for permitting me to see this introduction in manuscript.

47. "When Was *Huckleberry Finn* Written?" *AL*, XXX (March, 1958), 16.

48. Besides the pertinent sections in the major critical works, two articles are of special interest on this subject: O. H. Moore, "Mark Twain and *Don Quixote*," *PMLA*, XXXVII (1922), 324-46, and Walter Blair, "The French Revolution and *Huckleberry Finn*," *Modern Philology*, LV (August, 1957), 21-35.

49. *Love Letters*, p. 223.

50. Leo Marx, "Mr. Eliot, Mr. Trilling, and *Huckleberry Finn*," *American Scholar*, XXII (Autumn, 1953), 428.

51. Lionel Trilling, "Introduction," *Huckleberry Finn* (New York: Rinehart & Co., 1948), p. xv.

52. Marx, *op. cit.*, p. 428.

53. Trilling, *op. cit.*, pp. xv-xvi.

CHAPTER 5

1. *Mark Twain's Autobiography*, ed. A. B. Paine (hereafter *Autobiography*) (New York: Harper & Bros., 1924), I, 237-38.

2. G. W. Feinstein, "Mark Twain's Idea of Story Structure," *AL*, XVIII (May, 1946), 160-61.

3. *Autobiography*, II, 193. Such a narrative "plan" was in Mark Twain's mind as early as 1876. In her diary entry for April 27, 1876, Mrs. Fields quotes him as saying, "[The Autobiography] is to appear as it was written, with the whole tale told as truly as I can tell it.... But I shall not limit myself as to space, and at whatever age I am writing about, even if I am an infant, and an idea comes to me about myself when I am forty, I shall put that in" (Mrs. James T. Fields, *Memories of a Hostess*, ed. Mark A. DeWolfe Howe [Boston: Little, Brown & Co., 1922], p. 251). The implication is that Twain tried from 1876 to 1904 to *write* his autobiography, but without success.

4. Brander Matthews, "Memories of Mark Twain," in *The Tocsin of Revolt and Other Essays* (New York: Charles Scribner's Sons, 1922), pp. 265-66.

5. *Letters*, I, 267.

6. Walter Blair, "The French Revolution and *Huckleberry Finn*," *Modern Philology*, LV (August, 1957), 21.

7. *Love Letters*, p. 227.

8. Edgar H. Goold, "Mark Twain on the Writing of Fiction," *AL*, XXVI (May, 1954), 151.

9. *Notebook*, pp. 192-93.

10. Goold, *op. cit.*, p. 144.

11. *Ibid.*, p. 143.

12. DeVoto, *Mark Twain at Work*, p. 20.

13. Andrews, *op. cit.*, p. 214.

14. DeVoto, *Mark Twain at Work*, p. 52.

15. *Mark Twain in Eruption*, p. 199.

Bibliography

THE WRITINGS OF MARK TWAIN

The Adventures of Thomas Jefferson Snodgrass, ed. Charles Honce. Chicago: Pascal Covici, 1928.

The Celebrated Jumping Frog of Calaveras County and Other Sketches, ed. John Paul. New York: C. H. Webb, 1867.

Letters from the Sandwich Islands Written for the Sacramento Union, ed. G. Ezra Dane. Palo Alto: Stanford University Press, 1938.

The Love Letters of Mark Twain, ed. Dixon Wecter. New York: Harper & Bros., 1949.

Mark Twain in Eruption, ed. Bernard DeVoto. New York: Harper & Bros., 1940.

Mark Twain of the Enterprise, ed. Henry Nash Smith. Berkeley: University of California Press, 1957.

Mark Twain: San Francisco Correspondent; Selections from His Letters to the Territorial Enterprise: 1865-1866, ed. Henry Nash Smith and Frederick Anderson. San Francisco: Book Club of California, 1957.

Mark Twain to Mrs. Fairbanks, ed. Dixon Wecter. San Marino: Huntington Library, 1949.

Mark Twain's Autobiography, ed. A. B. Paine. New York: Harper & Bros., 1924.

Mark Twain's Letters, ed. A. B. Paine. New York: Harper & Bros., c. 1917.

Mark Twain's Notebook, ed. A. B. Paine. New York: Harper & Bros., 1935.

Mark Twain's Travels with Mr. Brown, ed. Franklin Walker and G. Ezra Dane. New York: Alfred A. Knopf, 1940.

The Portable Mark Twain, ed. Bernard DeVoto. New York: Viking Press, 1946.

The Writings of Mark Twain, Author's National Edition, 25 vols. New York: Harper & Bros., c. 1899-1909.

Mark Twain Papers. General Library, University of California, Berkeley.

OTHER BOOKS

ARISTOTLE. *Poetics,* trans. and ed. T. A. Moxon. London: J. M. Dent & Sons (Everyman's Library), 1941.

ANDREWS, KENNETH R. *Nook Farm, Mark Twain's Hartford Circle.* Cambridge: Harvard University Press, 1950.

BELLAMY, GLADYS C. *Mark Twain as a Literary Artist.* Norman: University of Oklahoma Press, 1950.

BRANCH, EDGAR M. *The Literary Apprenticeship of Mark Twain, With Selections from His Apprentice Writing.* Urbana: University of Illinois Press, 1950.

BROOKS, VAN WYCK. *The Ordeal of Mark Twain.* New York: Meridian Books, 1955.

BROWN, T. ALLSTON. *A History of the New York Stage.* 3 vols. New York: Dodd, Mead & Co., 1903.

BROWNE, J. ROSS. *A Dangerous Journey.* Palo Alto: A. Lites Press, 1950.

COMBE, WILLIAM. *Doctor Syntax's Three Tours: In Search of the Picturesque, Consolation, and a Wife.* London: John Camden Hotten, 1868.

CORTISSOZ, ROYAL. *Life of Whitelaw Reid.* New York: Charles Scribner's Sons, 1921.

COUSIN, VICTOR, C. JOURDAIN, et E. DESPOIS. *Petri Abaelardi Opera.* 2 vols. Paris: A. Durand, 1849-59.

CUTTER, BLOODGOOD H. *The Long Island Farmer's Poems.* New York: N. Tibbals & Sons, 1886.

DEVOTO, BERNARD A. *Mark Twain at Work.* Cambridge: Harvard University Press, 1942.

————. *Mark Twain's America.* Boston: Little, Brown & Co., 1932.

DICKENS, CHARLES. *David Copperfield.* New York: Random House (Modern Library College Editions), 1950.

DICKINSON, LEON T. "Mark Twain's *Innocents Abroad:* Its Origins, Composition and Popularity." Unpublished dissertation, University of Chicago, 1945.

DISTURNELL, J. *Sailing on the Great Lakes and Rivers of America.* Philadelphia: J. Disturnell, 1874.

Don Caesar de Bazan, French's Standard Drama No. XVI. New York: Samuel French, n.d.

FIELDS, MRS. JAMES T. (ANNIE A.) *Memories of a Hostess; a Chronicle of Eminent Friendships Drawn Chiefly from the Diaries of Mrs. James T. Fields,* ed. Mark A. DeWolfe Howe. Boston: Little, Brown & Co., 1922.

FISCHER, HENRY W. *Abroad with Mark Twain and Eugene Field.* New York: N. L. Brown, 1922.

GREARD, VALLERY. *Lettres complètes d'Abélard et d'Héloïse.* Paris: Garnier Frères, 1870.

GUIZOT, FRANCOIS. *Abaelard et Héloïse,* nouv. edn. Paris: Didier et Cie, 1876.

HUGO, VICTOR M. *The Man Who Laughs.* Translated by William Young. New York: D. Appleton & Co., 1869.

JOHANNSEN, ALBERT. *The House of Beadle and Adams and its Dime and Nickel Novels; the Story of a Vanished Literature.* 2 vols. Norman: University of Oklahoma Press, 1950.

MATTHEWS, BRANDER. *The Tocsin of Revolt and Other Essays.* New York: Charles Scribner's Sons, 1922.

ODELL, GEORGE C. D. *Annals of the New York Stage.* 15 vols. New York: Columbia University Press, 1927-49.

PAINE, ALBERT B. *Mark Twain, A Biography; the Personal and*

Literary Life of Samuel Langhorne Clemens. 3 vols. New York: Harper & Bros., 1912.

PARRINGTON, VERNON L. *Main Currents in American Thought.* 3 vols. New York: Harcourt, Brace & Co., 1930.

POMEROY, EARL. *In Search of the Golden West: The Tourist in Western America.* New York: Alfred A. Knopf, 1957.

RÉVOIL, BÉNÉDICT. *Shooting and Fishing in the Rivers, Prairies, and Backwoods of North America.* Translated by the Chronicler. 2 vols. London: Tinsley Bros., 1865.

TAYLOR, BAYARD. *The Echo Club and Other Literary Diversions.* Boston: James R. Osgood, 1876.

TOMPKINS, EUGENE. *History of the Boston Theatre 1854-1901.* Boston: Houghton Mifflin Co., 1908.

WAGNER, HENRY R. *The Plains and the Rockies,* rev. and enl. by Charles L. Camp. San Francisco: Grabhorn Press, 1937.

WALKER, FRANKLIN. *San Francisco's Literary Frontier.* New York: Alfred A. Knopf, 1939.

WEBB, CHARLES HENRY. *John Paul's Book.* Hartford: Columbian Book Co., 1874.

―――. *Parodies in Prose and Verse.* New York: G. W. Carleton, 1876.

WECTER, DIXON. *Sam Clemens of Hannibal.* Boston: Houghton Mifflin Co., 1952.

WIGHT, O. W. *Lives and Letters of Abelard and Heloise.* 2d ed. New York: M. Doolady, 1861.

ARTICLES, INTRODUCTIONS, AND ESSAYS

BAETZHOLD, HOWARD G. "Mark Twain's *The Prince and the Pauper,*" *Notes and Queries,* I, n.s. (September, 1954), 401-3.

BLAIR, WALTER. "Burlesques in Nineteenth-Century American Humor," *AL,* II (November, 1930), 236-47.

―――. "On the Structure of *Tom Sawyer,*" *Modern Philology,* XXXVII (August, 1939), 75-88.

———. "The French Revolution and *Huckleberry Finn,*" *Modern Philology,* LV (August, 1957), 21-35.

———. "When Was *Huckleberry Finn* Written?" *AL,* XXX (March, 1958), 1-25.

BRANCH, EDGAR M. "The Two Providences: Thematic Form in 'Huckleberry Finn,'" *College English,* XI (January, 1950), 188-95.

DIBELIUS, WILHELM. "Zu den *Pickwick Papers,*" *Anglia,* XXXV (1912), 101-10.

FEINSTEIN, G. W. "Mark Twain's Idea of Story Structure," *AL,* XVIII (May, 1946), 160-63.

GOOLD, EDGAR H., JR. "Mark Twain on the Writing of Fiction," *AL,* XXVI (May, 1954), 141-53.

LEISY, ERNEST E. "Mark Twain's Part in *The Gilded Age,*" *AL,* VIII (January, 1937), 445-47.

MARX, LEO. "Mr. Eliot, Mr. Trilling, and *Huckleberry Finn,*" *American Scholar,* XXII (Autumn, 1953), 423-40.

MOORE, OLIN H. "Mark Twain and *Don Quixote,*" *PMLA,* XXXVII (1922), 324-46.

ROGERS, FRANKLIN R. "Washoe's First Literary Journal," *California Historical Society Quarterly,* XXXVI (December, 1957), 365-70.

"Sketches on the Upper Mississippi," *Harper's New Monthly Magazine,* VII (July, 1853), 177-90.

SMITH, HENRY NASH. "Mark Twain as an Interpreter of the Far West," in *The Frontier in Perspective,* ed. Walker D. Wyman and Clifton B. Kroeber. Madison: University of Wisconsin Press, 1957.

———. "Introduction," *Huckleberry Finn.* Boston: Houghton Mifflin Co., 1958.

TRILLING, LIONEL. "Introduction," *Huckleberry Finn.* New York: Rinehart & Co., 1948.

Index

Ada Clare, *pseud.; see* McElheney, Jane
Adventures of Huckleberry Finn, 7, 13, 14, 96, 124, 126, 127-51, 154, 155, 156, 158, 159, 160-61; burlesque episodes in, 144-46; character-axis in, 139-42; contradictions in Huck, 142-44, 150; first narrative-plank of, 128-29; function of burlesque in, 146-48; moral pilgrimage in, 136-38; probability in, 149; raftsman's episode, 174-75 n. 45; second narrative-plank of, 129-35; structural flaw in, 148-51; three manuscript states of, 128; three structural stages of, 127-28; third narrative-plank of, 135-39; unfinished murder plot in, 130-31
Adventures of Tom Sawyer, 9, 13, 14, 96, 97-98, 101-13, 122, 123, 125, 126, 127, 128, 129, 140, 154, 155, 158, 159, 160; as burlesque of model-boy literature, 106-7; character-axis in, 110-12; narrative-plank of, 106-9; probability in, 112-13
Ainsworth, Harrison, 9
Aldrich, Thomas Bailey, 20
Alta California (San Francisco newspaper), 42
Alta California letters, 42-43, 44, 49, 51, 52, 54, 82, 85, 169 n. 42; character-axis in, 42; contrasting episodes in, 43
Andrews, Kenneth R., 90
Artemus Ward, *pseud.; see* Browne, Charles F.
Arthur, Timothy Shay, 100

Auerbach, Berthold, 86-87
"Aurelia's Unfortunate Young Man," 22
Austen, Jane, 9, 11, 12
Autobiography, 152-54, 175 n. 3
Autobiography of a Damn Fool, 128, 136
"Awful, Terrible Medieval Romance," 100-101

Ballou, John, 72-73
Barney the Baron (theatrical extravaganza), 105
Beadle and Adams (publishers), 68, 76
Bellamy, Gladys C., 4-5
Bennett, Emerson, 64, 68
Blair, Walter, 104, 106, 108, 127, 128, 133, 136, 138, 155
"Bloody Massacre," 73-74
Bohemians, 10, 14-16, 17-25, 28, 31, 93
Boucicault, Dion, 9, 18, 173 n. 29
"Boy's Manuscript, The," 20, 97-98, 101-6, 108, 112
Brackenridge, Hugh Henry, 165 n. 9
Braddon, Mrs. Mary E., 9, 77
Branch, Edgar M., 5-6, 9
Brooks, Van Wyck, 7-8, 163 n. 7
Browne, Charles F. (Artemus Ward, *pseud.*), 15-16, 17, 18
Browne, J. Ross, 69, 165 n. 9
Buffalo Express (newspaper), 100, 114
Bulletin (San Francisco newspaper), 21
Bulwer-Lytton, Edward George Earle Lytton, first Baron Lytton, 78

185